A
LISTENING

DISCARD

Brother David Steindl-Rast

A
LISTENING
HEART

THE SPIRITUALITY OF SACRED SENSUOUSNESS

Newly Revised

A Crossroad Book
The Crossroad Publishing Company
New York

The Crossroad Publishing Company
370 Lexington Avenue, New York, NY 10017

Printed in the United States of America

Library of Congress Cataloging-in-Publication Data

Steindl-Rast, David.
    A listening heart : the spirituality of sacred sensuousness / David
Steindl-Rast. — [Rev. ed.]
        p.   cm.
    Includes bibliographical references.
    ISBN 0-8245-1780-6 (pbk.)
    1. Spiritual life — Catholic Church. 2. Sensuality —
Religious aspects — Catholic Church. I. Title.
BX2350.65.S75   1999
248.4'82 — dc21   99–34367
                                                 CIP

The Publisher gratefully acknowledges permission to use the following copyrighted material:

"The Environment as Guru" originally appeared in *Cross Currents,* vol. 24 nos. 2-3 (1973). Used with permission.
"A Deep Bow" originally appeared in *Main Currents XXIII,* no. 5 (1967). Used with permission.
Excerpts from *Four Quartets* by T. S. Eliot reprinted by permission of Faber and Faber Ltd.
Excerpts from *Four Quartets* by T. S. Eliot reprinted by permission of Harcourt Brace Jovanovich, Inc.; Copyright © 1943 by T. S. Eliot, renewed 1971 by Esme Valerie Eliot.
Excerpts from *Candles in Babylon.* Copyright © 1982 by Denise Levertov. Reprinted by permission of New Directions Publishing Corp.
Excerpts from *Candles In Babylon* by Denise Levertov. Reprinted by permission of Laurence Pollinger Unlimited.
"Haiku" from *An Introduction to Haiku* by Harold G. Henderson. Copyright © 1958 by Harold G. Henderson. Reprinted by permission of Doubleday & Company, Inc.
Excerpts from *Duino Elegies* by Rainer Maria Rilke. Translated by J.B. Leishman/Stephen Spender. Translation copyright 1939 by W.W. Norton & Company, Inc., renewed © 1967 by Stephen Spender and J.B. Leishman. Reprinted by permission of W.W. Norton & Company Inc.
Excerpts from *Collected Poems 1909-1962* by T. S. Eliot reprinted by permission of Harcourt, Brace & World, Inc. Copyright © 1963.
Excerpts from *Collected Poems 1909-1962* by T.S. Eliot reprinted by permission of Faber and Faber Ltd.
Excerpts from *Samtiche Werke* Vol. I by R. M. Rilke reprinted by permission of Frankfurt: Insel-Verlag: Copyright © 1962.
Excerpts from *Woods* by Noelle Oxenhandler reprinted with permission of the author.
"The Guitarist Tunes Up" from *On a Calm Shore* by Frances Cornford. Copyright ©1921 by Frances Cornford. Reprinted by permission of the Cresset Press.

    2   3   4   5   6   7   8   9   10   04   03   02   01   99

May this new version of *A Listening Heart* be a token of my gratitude for the listening hearts of friends, especially

NANCY L. GRAEFF

and all others who helped with professional skill, advice, support, and constructive criticism. *

I am deeply grateful also for the listening hearts of my readers.

* Snjezana Bakula, Mel Bricker, Joan Casey, Michael Casey, Lorilott Clark, Brendan Collins, Sandy Conheim, Judy Dunbar, Christine Gunn, Gwendolyn Herder, Kateri Kautai, Paul Kobelski, Paul Lacey, Matthew Laughlin, Chris Lorenc, Laura Martin, Sajid Martin, David Schulz, Michaela Terrio, Daniel Uvanovic, Margaret van Kempen O.S.B.

Contents

Introduction

Brother David Steindl-Rast is an authentic monk. Like the Buddhist monk Thich Nhat Hanh, whom he cites in this book, Brother David is able to communicate simple living and simple seeing to the rest of us who are in the world looking for meaning and spiritual support as we struggle to pay our bills, raise our families, face our trials, fight our ethical battles and just plain live.

What makes an authentic monk? I think clarity of mind and sight, simplicity of life and gratitude in the heart. In short, what Brother David calls a "listening heart."

It takes self-knowledge and freedom from projection to render the heart a listening one. The monk listens. All of us do (or ought to). The monk might be called a professional listener. Maybe we all should be professional listeners.

For there is so much that is being said in the universe and in our hearts that deserves silent attention — some of it is the music of beauty and awe and wonder; and some of it is the lamentation of grief and anger, sadness and sorrow. All of it deserves our listening. And Brother David in this book gives us ample lessons in how to enrich our listening.

At this time of an emerging millennium (and an ending one), when the planet is being despoiled by so much

Introduction

reckless human encroachment of its natural systems of checks and balances, and in this time when Christianity seeks to simplify itself and to return to the spirit of Jesus and the Christ-awareness that Jesus knew so well, certain monks are being asked to share the fruits of their listening heart with others. Thich Nhat Hanh, the Dalai Lama and Pema Chodron are examples of persons responding to this call from the East; Brother David is a fine example from the West. Indeed, these people are on similar paths. Though their journeys started differently — three with the Buddha, Brother David with Christ — their paths have crossed. Intersection is happening a lot these days. The young recognize it. Cultural pluralism and religious pluralism and spiritual pluralism are signs of our times. And Brother David is a leader in this work of spiritual ecumenism and of science reconnecting to spirituality and of rescuing the essence of the Christian message, what Meister Eckhart called "the kernel," from the historical Jesus and from his monastic tradition and practices.

In this book we readers are the grateful and fortunate recipients of Brother David's wisdom. Brother David walks his talk and he sings his silence. Like his Benedictine Sister Hildegard of Bingen, whose 900th anniversary we celebrate this year, he seeks wisdom over knowledge and in preference to folly and he makes our hearts greener and wetter and more creative and joyful.

Time and again Brother David returns to the key theme of *gratitude* in this book. He is so wise to do so. If our species were truly grateful, would we be despoiling the very beauty and health of this planet as we are? Or would we be so often seduced by luxury life-styles or consumer addictions if we had learned what the real *graces* in life are? ("Grace" and "gratitude" come from the very same root word.) With Meister Eckhart, Brother David's message could be summarized as follows: If the only prayer you say in your whole life is "Thank You," that would suffice.

Brother David knows his Benedictine tradition well and knows it was based on a Biblical, original blessing theology more than an original sin ideology. In this book he instructs us in a holy and sensuous asceticism that does not flee the body or the body politic but *inspires* both. This book breathes spirit and life into persons and community.

When he declares that "every sensuous experience is at heart a spiritual one: a divine revelation," Brother David calls us to our senses again. Our holy senses. He calls us to the very basic meaning of mysticism, to "enter the mysteries," and he demonstrates how our senses are indeed gateways to Spirit and not obstacles to Spirit as some guilt-producing theologians have suggested they were over the centuries. Brother David redefines "asceticism," insisting that an authentically Incarnational Christian theology ought to speak of "sensuous asceticism." This represents a giant step forward since during the mechanistic modern era the term "asceticism" pretty much degenerated into a kind of mechanical way of treating and indeed abusing our senses for the sake of a perceived spiritual purity. Our senses are meant to serve the heart — "our ears hear, but only a listening heart understands." Yet we are meant to go beyond sensual pleasure to a joy that lasts.

I am grateful for this deep and profound book, as I am sure many other readers will be also. It tells truths of the spiritual life that need telling and it tells them with

Introduction

story and poems and humor — a style that deserves our attention. The author speaks not from the lofty pinnacles of a pulpit preacher or an academic savant, but from the inside to the inside, that is from listening heart to listening heart. To get the most from this book one must listen with one's heart.

I hope we are listening — young and old alike. For the future of our species and of the planet's beauty and health and diversity as we know it depends on what we humans choose to do with our hearts. If we can let go and cleanse our hearts, learning to listen deeply again, then there is hope. To listen with gratitude, and grow in the reverence and wonder that grows from gratitude, and grow in our capacities for not-taking-for-granted. In this sense, Brother David invites all of us to be mystics again and prophets, too, that our joy may flow over into our work in the world. In this way, not only Eastern and Western wisdom, theological and scientific knowledge, but also the monastic and lay worlds may melt together so that all may be one and in this great "one-ing" we may together recover community and celebration, justice-making and healing. This would surely be a blessing and return us to a sense of original blessing. A time of true community celebration and gratitude would follow. Reverence for all being would be the result. And still more of creation would join the celebration.

Matthew Fox
University of Creation Spirituality
Oakland, California

Not a Foreword

Dear Casual Browser,

This is NOT A FOREWORD, just a brief note to you. Writing a book is a chore; finishing it is gratifying; seeing it published is a joy. Now imagine what joy it is for me that sixteen years after it first came out, *A Listening Heart* is still finding a steady stream of readers. Better still: readers tell me they find this teenager of mine a helpful kid. This pleases a parent, I readily admit. Less readily, I must admit that this offspring of mine was not the result of Planned Parenthood. In fact, at first sight I didn't even recognize my baby.

As it happened, I had just returned from a long lecture tour down under when, after a lecture back home again, someone handed me a book to sign. Noting my surprised look, she explained, "You wrote it!"

Did I? Well, in a sense I did — not as a book, though. A well-meaning friend had put together essays of mine and turned them into this book. While grateful, I was also embarrassed. A "listening heart" is indeed a key topic for me, but the essays didn't all fit this theme equally well, nor did they develop it consistently. So, when I was asked to prepare a German translation, I replaced the middle section with new chapters. In this revised edition, I have done the same for English readers. Now I am satisfied — as satisfied as a dyed-in-the-wool perfectionist can be.

Nothing essential to the topic was lost; much, I feel, was gained. The two eliminated chapters on contemplative life and community were too sketchy. I hope to expand them into a separate book. Instead I am offering here something fresh: a Christian spirituality that celebrates sensuous pleasure and a spiritual practice to match it.

A spirituality based on original blessing (as opposed to one fixated on original sin) has been making promising noises lately, like a fiery stallion whinnying and pawing the ground. This new version of *A Listening Heart* invites you to get in the saddle of that life-affirming spirituality and gallop away.

A Listening Heart

The key word of the spiritual discipline I follow is "listening." This means a special kind of listening, a listening with one's heart. To listen in that way is central to the monastic tradition in which I stand. The very first word of the Rule of St. Benedict is "Listen!" — *"Ausculta!"* — and all the rest of Benedictine discipline grows out of this one initial gesture of wholehearted listening, as a sunflower grows from its seed.

Benedictine spirituality in turn is rooted in the broader and more ancient tradition of the Bible. But here, too, the concept of listening is central. In the biblical vision all things are brought into existence by God's creative Word; all of history is a dialogue with God, who speaks to the human heart. The Bible has been admired for proclaiming with great clarity that God is One and Transcendent. Yet, the still more admirable insight of the religious genius reflected in biblical literature is the insight that God speaks. The transcendent God communicates Self through nature and through history. The human heart is called to listen and to respond.

Responsive listening is the form the Bible gives to our basic religious quest as human beings. This is the quest for a full human life, for happiness. It is the quest for meaning, for our happiness hinges not on good luck: it hinges on peace of heart. Even in the midst of what we call bad luck, even in the midst of pain and suffering, we can find peace of heart, if we find meaning in it all. Biblical tradition points the way by proclaiming that God speaks to us in and through even the most troublesome predicaments. By listening deeply to the message of any given moment I shall be able to tap the very Source of Meaning and to realize the unfolding meaning of my life.

To listen in this way means to listen with one's heart, with one's whole being. The heart stands for that center of our being at which we are truly "together." Together with ourselves, not split up into intellect, will, emotions, into mind and body. Together with all other creatures, for the heart is that realm where I am paradoxically not only most intimately myself, but most intimately united with all. Together with God, the source of life, the life of my life, welling up in my heart. In order to listen with my heart, I must return again and again to my heart through a process of centering, through taking things to heart. Listening with my heart I will find meaning. For just as the eye perceives light and the ear sound, the heart is the organ for meaning.

The most original insight of the Bible is that "God speaks" to us through nature and history.

The daily discipline of listening and responding to meaning is called obedience. This concept of obedience is far more comprehensive than the narrow notion of obedience as doing-what-you-are-told-to-do. Obedience in the full sense is the process of attuning the heart to the simple call contained in the complexity of a given situation. The only alternative is absurdity. *Ab-surdus* literally means absolutely deaf. If I call a situation absurd I admit that I am deaf to its meaning. I admit implicitly that I must become *ob-audiens* — thoroughly listening, obedient. I must give my ear, give myself, so fully to the word that reaches me that it will send me. Being sent by the word, I will be obedient to my mission. Thus, by doing the truth lovingly, not by analyzing it, I will begin to understand.

The ethical implications of all this are obvious. Therefore it is all the more important to remember that we are not primarily concerned with an ethical but with a religious matter; not primarily with purpose, even the most exalted purpose of good works, but with that religious dimension from which every purpose must derive its meaning. The Bible calls the responsive listening of obedience "living by the Word of God," and that means far more than merely doing God's will. It means being nourished by God's word as food and drink, God's word in every person, every thing, every event.

This is a daily task, a moment by moment discipline. I eat a tangerine and the resistance of the rind, as I peel it, speaks to me, if I am alert enough. Its texture, its fragrance speak an untranslatable language, which I have to learn. Beyond the awareness that each little segment has its own degree of sweetness (the ones on the side that was exposed to the sun are the sweetest) lies the awareness that all this is pure gift. Or could one ever deserve such food?

I hold a friend's hand in mine, and this gesture becomes a word, the meaning of which goes far beyond words. It makes demands on me. It is an implicit pledge. It calls for faithfulness and for sacrifice. But it is above all a celebration of friendship, a meaningful gesture that need not be justified by any practical purpose. It is as superfluous as a sonnet or a string quartet, as superfluous as all the ultimately important things in life. It is a word of God by which I live.

But a calamity is also a word of God when it hits me. While working for me, a young man, as dear to me as my own little brother, has an accident. Glass is shattered in his eyes, and I find him lying blindfolded in a hospital bed. What is God saying now? Together we grope, grapple, listen, strain to hear. Is this, too, a life-giving word? When we can no longer make sense of a given situation, we have reached the crucial point. Now arises the challenge that calls for faith.

The clue lies in the fact that any given moment confronts us with a given reality. But if it is given, it is gift. If it is gift, the appropriate response is thanksgiving. Yet, thanksgiving, where it is genuine, does not primarily look at the gift and express appreciation; it looks at the giver and expresses trust. The courageous confidence that trusts in the Giver of all gifts is faith. To give thanks even when we cannot see the goodness of the Giver — to learn this is to find the path to peace of heart. For happiness is not what makes us grateful. It is gratefulness that makes us happy.

In a lifelong process the discipline of listening teaches us to live by *every* word that proceeds from the mouth of God without discrimination. We learn this by "giving thanks in *all* things." The monastery is an environment set up to facilitate just that. The method is detachment. When we fail to distinguish between wants and needs we lose sight of our goal. Our needs (many of them imaginary) keep increasing; our gratefulness (and so our happiness) dwindles. Monastic discipline reverses this course. The monk strives for needing less and less while becoming more and more grateful.

Detachment decreases our needs. The less we have, the easier it is gratefully to appreciate what we do have. Silence creates the atmosphere for detachment. Silence pervades monastic life in the same way in which noise pervades life elsewhere. Silence creates space around things, persons, and events. Silence singles them out and allows us gratefully to consider them one by one in their uniqueness. Leisure is the discipline of finding time to do so. Leisure is the expression of detachment with regard to time. For the leisure of monks is not the privilege of those who can afford to take time; it is the virtue of those who give to everything they do the time it deserves to take.

Our heart is that center where we are one with ourselves, with all others, and with God.

Within the monastery the listening which is the essence of this spiritual discipline expresses itself in bringing life into harmony with the cosmic rhythm of seasons and hours, with "time, not our time" as T. S. Eliot calls it. But in my personal life, obedience often demands that I serve outside the monastery. What counts is the listening to the soundless bell of "time, not our time," wherever it be and the doing of whatever needs to be done when it is time — "now, and in the hour of our death." "And the time of death is every moment," says T. S. Eliot, because the moment in which we truly listen is "a moment in and out of time."

A Listening Heart

One method for entering moment by moment into that mystery is the discipline of the Jesus Prayer, the Prayer of the Heart, as it is also called. It consists basically in the mantric repetition of the name of Jesus, synchronized with one's breath and heartbeat. When I repeat the name of Jesus at a given moment in time, I make that moment transparent to the Now that does not pass away. The whole biblical notion of living by the Word is summed up in the name of Jesus in whom I as a Christian adore the Word incarnate. By giving that name to every thing and to every person I encounter, by invoking it in every situation in which I find myself, I remind myself that everything is just another way of spelling out the inexhaustible fullness of the one eternal word of God, the Logos; I remind my heart to listen! This image might seem to suggest a dualistic rift between God who speaks and the obedient heart. Yet, the dualistic tension is caught up and transcended in the mystery of the Trinity. In the light of that mystery I understand myself as a word spoken out of the Creator's heart and at the same time addressed by the Creator. But the communion goes deeper. In order to understand the word addressed to me, the word I am, I must speak the language of the One who calls. If I can understand God at all this can come about only by my sharing in God's own Spirit of Self-understanding. Thus the responsive listening in which my spiritual discipline consists is not dualistic communica-

Eyes see only light, ears hear only sound, but a Listening Heart perceives meaning.

tion. It is the celebration of triune communion: the Word, coming forth from Silence, leads by Understanding home into Silence. My heart, like a vessel thrown into the ocean, is filled with God's life and totally immersed in it. All this is pure gift. It remains for me to rise to the occasion by an all-embracing thanksgiving.

The Environment as Guru

What I wish to share with you is aimed at making you feel at home in a monastery. We might begin with the question: "What should this environment do for us?" Maybe some of you have never been in a monastery; perhaps others have spent most of their lives in one. But it might be worthwhile for all of us to ask ourselves, "What is a monastery, actually?"

The easiest answer, of course, and probably the best, is to say, "Come and see!" And if one came quietly enough, one might find out much without any talk. If, however, we must speak about it, I would suggest that a monastery is, first of all, a controlled environment, with all the advantages and disadvantages included in this notion. It's inevitably a somewhat artificial environment, for a particular professional pursuit.

We know there are controlled environments for other professional pursuits. The monastery is a controlled environment for the professional pursuit of cultivating one's contemplative dimension. Those who live in a monastery have made this their profession. They have made public profession of dedicating themselves radically to the task of cultivating that contemplative dimension, which in fact belongs to every one of us. If we call monks the professionals of the contemplative life, this does not mean that they are better at it than amateurs may be.

We all know that very often, when you need your sink fixed, an amateur plumber will do a much better job than a professional. That someone is a professional does not mean that he or she is better at the relevant professional skills; but it does mean that one ought to try harder. When we say that monks are professionals, therefore, we are saying that they have accepted the responsibility of cultivating professionally what many enjoy merely as amateurs, the contemplative dimension.

But what do we mean by "contemplative"? If we follow our own particular tradition as Benedictine monks and trace the very word to its Latin root, we may come to see an aspect of contemplation that might complement those that stand more in the foreground of other traditions. I stress this because Father Damasus, the founder of Mount Saviour monastery, used to consider it of great importance; in our tradition the notion of contemplation hinges on the Latin word *contemplari*. The image and, originally, the reality that stands behind this notion, is that of the Roman augurs, who marked off a particular area in the sky, the *templum*. Originally, *templum* was not a building on the ground but an area in the skies on which the augurs, professional seers, fixed their eyes in order to find the immutable order according to which matters here below should be arranged. The sacred order of the temple is merely the reflection of the sacred order above. Father Damasus kept stressing the fact that contemplation consists in the bringing together of the two temples, as the *con* in *contemplari* suggests.

Along with this Roman notion there is the biblical pattern: Moses built the sanctuary exactly according to the vision shown him by God on the mountain. Again and again the Bible stresses the faithful correspondence between the temple on earth and its heavenly exemplar. In this sense, Moses truly fulfills the role of the contemplative. And not by chance: what he attempted and what the augurs attempted springs from the same root. The contemplative gesture is deeply rooted in our heart and in our longing for universal harmony. Through the ages humans have longingly looked up to the harmony and order of the starry universe, attuning their heartbeat to its measured movement.

Contemplation attunes our heartbeat to the rhythm of the universe.

Measure seems to be the basic meaning of the linguistic root from which stem not only cognates like temperature, temperament, template and temporality, but, of course, temple and contemplation. To measure one's step by a universal rhythm and thus to bring one's life into harmony with a universal order — this is *contemplatio* in our tradition.

To move in step, one needs to listen; to sight one's course, one needs to look. The monastery is, therefore, conceived as a place where one learns to keep one's eyes and ears open. "Listen!" is the first word of St. Benedict's Rule for Monasteries, and another keyword is "consider!" — literally meaning to lay your course by the stars. St. Benedict, the patriarch of Western monks, wants them to live *apertis oculis* and *attonitis auribus,* with open eyes, and with ears so alert that the silence of God's presence sounds like thunder. This is why a Benedictine monastery is to be a *schola Dominici servitii*, a school in which one learns to attune oneself to ultimate order.

But such an order means nothing rigid. That would be the great danger, that would be the trap into which one could fall, to conceive of ultimate order as static. On the contrary, it is profoundly dynamic; the only image that we can ultimately find for this order is the dance of the spheres. What we are invited to do, what we are to learn in the monastery, professionally, is to listen to that tune, to attune ourselves to that harmony to which the whole universe dances. St. Augustine expresses the dynamism of order when he says, *"Ordo est amoris,"* which means that order is simply the expression of the love that moves the universe, Dante's *l'amor che muove il sole è l'altre stelle.* But the fact is that while the rest of the universe moves freely and gracefully in cosmic harmony, we humans don't. It costs us an effort to attune ourselves to the dynamic order of love. At some point it even costs the supreme effort of, yes, making no effort. The obstacle which we must overcome is attachment, even the attachment to our own effort. Asceticism is the professional approach to overcoming attachment in all its forms. Our image of the dance should help us understand it. Detachment, which is merely its negative aspect, frees our movements, helps make us nimble. The positive aspect of asceticism is alertness, wakefulness, aliveness. As we become free to move, we begin to learn the steps; to listen to the music, listen and respond.

Asceticism (in its negative aspect) may thus be understood as training in detachment for the sake of being in tune with universal harmony (the positive goal). But if this harmony is to be truly universal, it must encompass

11

all of reality. If contemplation aims at "bringing the two temples together," all of reality must become transparent to its innermost luminous structure, and ultimate order must find its expression in space and in time. Asceticism must, therefore, cultivate its own environment, as well as its awareness of space and time, as a form of obedience to the environment as guru.

If I understand it correctly, the word *guru* means "dispeller of darkness." Not in the sense that there is something light and good, and something bad and dark. No, reality is not split in two. Let us understand dispelling of darkness in its symbolic sense as the dispelling of confusion. If it is the guru's function to dispel confusion — beginning with the confusion that there are two parts to reality — the result will be order. Only let us keep in mind that it is the dynamic order of life and love, the mysterious order of the great dance. The various traditions have developed a great variety of forms for learning to put one's life in order — into such order. Prominent among these forms is what we might call an environmental asceticism of space and time.

Both in our tradition and in others, asceticism of space, the training in detachment as it relates to any given place, centers on learning to be present where we are. This is the first step: and how often do we fail in it! We are ahead of ourselves or are hanging behind. Part of us is stretching out to a future that is not yet, part is hanging on to a past that is no more. What is left of us is not truly present either. We are here and not here, because we are not awake. To be present where we are means to wake up to this place.

In the Judeo-Christian tradition a classical locus for insights regarding the asceticism of space is the spiritual exegesis of the scene in which Moses confronts the Burning Bush. The voice out of the Bush calls to him, "Take off your shoes! This is holy ground." To take off one's shoes — this is the asceticism of space. To take off one's shoes means being truly there, fully alive. The shoes or sandals we take off are made from the skin of dead animals. As long as we wear them, there is something dead between the live soles of our feet and the ground on which we are standing. To take off this deadness means taking off that familiarity which breeds contempt and boredom: it means coming alive in primordial freshness to the place where we are.

At first it is a specific place, the sacred precinct, which we enter barefoot. But then comes the next step, the decisive one: you come to realize that wherever you take off your shoes, you stand on holy ground. "All around in every direction: Holy of Holies" (Ez. 45:1), a passage Father Damasus never tired of quoting to his monks. All you have to do is to "take off your shoes" and you

Any place is sacred ground, for it can become a place of encounter with the divine Presence.

will realize this. In the Benedictine tradition this insight determines the attitude required toward every detail of the environment. The Rule of St. Benedict is concise to the point of being abrupt, yet it devotes an amazing number of passages to the various parts of the environment: the architectural layout, the use of tools, the food and clothing of the monks, the furnishings of the monastery. The final proof comes when St. Benedict says that every pot and pan in the monastery should be treated like the sacred vessels of the altar. This means: Take off your shoes and recognize that you are standing on sacred ground; this whole place is a temple.

Any place is sacred ground, because it is, potentially, a place of confrontation — confrontation with the divine Presence. As soon as we take off the shoes of "being used to it" and come alive, we realize: "If not here, where? When, if not now?" Nowhere if not now/here, we are confronted with Ultimate Reality. "In the fields or on a journey, in whatever place the monks may find themselves when it is time to pray, let them reverently bend their knees then and there," enjoins the Holy Rule. And thus the asceticism of place opens up toward the asceticism of time. To the here, the holy ground, belongs the now, the Kairos, the holy moment, the acceptable time, the today of which we sing in the liturgy over and over again. "Today, when you hear his voice, harden not your hearts" — a decisive passage. And this today is always.

Time is not clock-time, but opportunity — opportunity to wake up to the timeless now.

Time is something entirely different in the monastic context from that which a chronometer could measure. Time is not ours. When T. S. Eliot says, "Time, not our time," he points toward true detachment from time. We claim to have time, gain time, save time; in reality time does not belong to us. It is measured not by the clock, but by when it is time. That is why bells are so important in a monastery. Bells are a great help in getting monks out of bed early. No one will deny the importance of that. But the really important thing is that in a monastery we do things not when we feel like it, but when it is time. When the bell rings, St. Benedict wants the monk to put down his pen without crossing his "t" or dotting his "i." Such is the asceticism of time.

There are occasions when it is time for something, whether you like it or not. And if you come only five minutes late, the sun is not going to re-rise for you; it is not going to re-set for you; and noon is not going to come a little later because you turned the clock back. Those are decisive moments, around which the whole monastic day revolves — moments that the bell indicates, not just the arbitrary time of some timetable someone has made up. Let all these bells which you will hear ringing remind you that it is *time,* not *our* time.

The moment we let go of our time, all time is ours. We are beyond time, because we are in the present moment, in the now which transcends time. The now is not in time. If any of us know what now means, we know something that goes beyond time. For certainly the future is not, it has not yet come; and certainly the past is not, it is no more. So we say, "Well, but now is." But, when is the now? Is it in time? How long does this now last? Assign the shortest span of time to the now — you can still divide it in half: one half for the future, one half for the past. Is the dividing line then the now? As long as it remains a span of time, you can divide it again and again, *ad infinitum.* And so we find that in time there is only the seam between a past that is no more and a future that is not yet; and the now is not in time at all. Now is beyond time. And we humans are the only ones who know what

15

now means, because we exist, we "stick out" of time. That's what it means to exist. And all those monastic bells are simply reminders for us: now! — and that's all.

To get through this asceticism of space and time from confusion to order, to harmony of darkness and light — that's what we try to do at the monastery. Of course, we cannot claim to have accomplished it. To quote Eliot again:

> For most of us, this is the aim
> Never here to be realized;
> Who are only undefeated
> Because we have gone on trying....
>
> *The Dry Salvages, V*

> For us, there is only the trying. The rest is
> Not our business.
> *— East Coker, V*

We are trying to enter into that asceticism of space and time, to open ourselves to the environment as the dispeller of darkness, i.e., confusion, thereby finding peace.

Our Latin tradition defines peace as *tranquillitas ordinis,* the stillness of order. Order is inseparable from silence, but this is a dynamic silence. The tranquility of order is a dynamic tranquility, the stillness of a flame burning in perfect calm, of a wheel spinning so fast that it seems to stand still. Silence in this sense is not only a quality of the environment, but primarily an attitude, an attitude of listening. This is a gift that each of us is invited to give all others: the gift of silence. Let us, then, give one another silence. And let us begin right now.

The Environment as Guru

Let us give to one another that gift of silence, so that we can listen together and listen to one another. Only in this silence will we be able to hear that gentle breath of peace, that music to which the spheres dance, that universal harmony to which we, too, hope to dance.

Sacred Sensuousness
A Step-by-Step Approach

Delight in sense experience has often received a bad press. Some have put down sensual enjoyment because they thought this was the proper religious attitude. Jesus did not share this attitude. But then, Jesus was not much concerned with being proper. He showed such zest for life that respectable members of society called him "a glutton and a wine-bibber" (Mt. 11:19). Their own strait-laced stance appeared to them as the truly religious one. In contrast, the friends of Jesus experienced in his company through all their senses God's liberating presence. In the inflection and modulation of his voice God's message reached their ears. What he said was inseparable from how he said it. As his hands touched their skin, God's caring touched their hearts. From there it was only a small step to the insight that every sensuous experience is at heart a spiritual one, a divine revelation. No matter how we repress this intuition, it is there in every human heart just waiting to be triggered.

God's Good News comes to us humans first and foremost through our senses: "Our message concerns that which was from the beginning. We have heard it; we have seen it with our own eyes; we have looked at it and our hands have touched it: the life-giving Word. ... We bear witness to what we have seen and heard ... so that your joy may be complete" (1 Jn. 1:1-4).

Joy is the gist of the Christian Good News. Yet, only if we open wide our senses will we be able to drink from the source of this joy. Only then will the Good News prove truly good and ever new.

Common sense tells us there is nothing in our intellect that did not enter through the doors of perception. Our loftiest concepts are rooted in sense experiences. Only by going to their roots can we "dig" great ideas. People who are too fastidious to dirty their hands by coming to grips with concepts at their roots are left with notions that are literally "cut and dried." Cut off from the senses, dry reasoning turns into non-sense.

We must, of course, distinguish between sensuousness and sensuality. The difference is that sensuality gets so wrapped up in sensual pleasure that it never goes on to find full joy. A life rooted in sensuousness thrives. A life entangled in sensuality chokes and withers; it resembles a tangle of roots. Healthy sensuousness rises from root to vine to leaf and fragrant blossom. The sweet scent of honeysuckle in the evening air could not exist without the vine's hidden roots; but now this surpassing fragrance has its own existence. True joy surpasses mere sensuous pleasure. Without ever rejecting our senses we must go beyond them. Sooner or later, our senses wilt and die. True joy lasts. We shall have to say more about this, in a separate chapter on asceticism.

For now, let us emphasize this: to be alienated from our senses means being alienated from what is truly human. How is it possible for someone to get trapped in such alienation? We need to tackle this basic question head-on. Our human condition is such that from the start we run the risk of developing a split in our consciousness. This has to do with our relationship to the body. On the one hand, we look into a mirror and say, "This is me," while all we see is a body. On the other hand, we say with equal conviction, "I have a body." How can you *be* this body and at the same time *have,* own, possess it? Obviously you are somebody, yet you know that you are more than just some body.

The taste of wild strawberries, a toothache, or the pleasure rippling all over your skin after a bath — without a doubt, these are bodily experiences. But can you say this with the same assurance about homesickness, faithfulness, or the awe you feel as you look at the photograph of a spiral galaxy, say the Andromeda Nebula, two million light years from Earth and 200,000 light years in diameter?

We humans belong to both realms, the realm of the senses and a realm that goes beyond them. This stretches us. To avoid the tension of this stretching process we are apt to settle for half of our rightful inheritance. Still, our human birth gives us a dual citizenship. Only by claiming both realms as home can we avoid the polarization of our human consciousness. Our noblest task is to make the most of this creative tension. If we neglect what goes beyond our senses, we sink below animals. But if we deny being animals and neglect or reject our senses, we clip the very wings on which we are meant to rise to higher spheres. Unless we claim our dual citizenship and are at home with both angels and beasts we become alienated from both, alienated from what is truly human; we become — in Christopher Fry's apt image, "half-witted angels strapped to the backs of mules."

In striking contrast to this image stands another one found in St. Mark's Gospel. Mark draws with a few strokes an icon of human fulfillment, when he says of Jesus, "He was among animals and angels served him" (Mk. 1:13). Mark's terse account of Jesus' forty-day vision quest in the wilderness points backwards to its roots in Psalm 91. There God's upright one is protected from wild beasts by ministering angels. But Mark's passage points forward to its fruits as well. It anticipates the countless upright ones who went into the wilderness in search of spiritual fulfillment. Legends about these Desert Saints tell of their pulling thorns out of lions' paws, of stags fleeing to them for protection from hunters, of ravens bringing them food. Much of this may be fiction, but the ideal remains as a fact — the ideal of human beings living in peace with nature and supernature. The Desert Saints lived in communion with animals and so they lived also in communion with angels.

True sensuousness rises on the wings of the senses and so finds sense — meaning.

As human beings we stand at the crossroads of body and mind, of senses and sense. To hold these opposite poles together in harmony is our existential task. Now and then, someone accomplishes this task and the result shines forth as uniquely human beauty: a body radiant with brightness from beyond the senses; intangible splendor yet fully embodied. The eyes of true lovers are lucid enough to see this beauty in each other; we catch

glimpses of it in great masterpieces of the visual arts; a piece of music may express it, or a poem, or a dancer's grace. The Austrian poet Rainer Maria Rilke, who wrote his *Duino Elegies* and *Sonnets to Orpheus* in the same year (1922) in which T. S. Eliot wrote *The Wasteland*, made our standing at the crossroads a central theme of his poetic work. For Rilke, we humans stand at the crossroads between animals and angels. Angels are in Rilke's mythic world view as completely at home in a realm beyond the senses, in "the invisible," as animals are in "the visible," the realm of the senses. Astride both domains stands Orpheus, representative of full human existence.

> Is he a local? No, from both
> regions stems his vast nature.
>
> *Sonnets to Orpheus, 1:6*

Being at home on both sides of the border, we humans are destined to be translators. We can teach angels who are eager to learn what only our animal senses can perceive. We humans alone can transform "the visible" into "the invisible." "We are transformers of the Earth," Rilke writes, "our whole existence ... fits us for this task (a task to which no other stands comparison)."

If you have ever watched a honeybee tussle and tumble about in the silky recesses of a peony blossom you will appreciate an image Rilke uses for our task of translating sense experience into experience that goes beyond the senses. Watch that bee revelling in the fragrance of innumerable purple and white and pink petals until, dusted with golden pollen, it finds the source of nectar hidden at the heart of the flower. Watch how with total absorption of all its senses in this peony world the bee performs what is both vital task and ecstatic play. And then read how the poet understands our own task in this human world:

> Our task is to impress on our whole being this passing, impermanent earth so deeply, so painfully and passionately, that it will rise again — now "invisible" — within us. We are the bees of the invisible. With total absorption, we gather the nectar of the visible into the great golden honeycomb of the invisible.
>
> (*Letter to W. v. Hulewicz*; Nov. 13, 1925)

This visible and this invisible meet at the crossroads which we call our heart. When we say "heart," we mean that center of our personal being where we are one with ourselves; yet, not with ourselves only. In our heart of hearts we are one also with all others — all humans, animals, plants, the whole cosmos — and with the Ultimate, with God. St. Augustine affirms from his own mystical awareness a truth of which every human being has an inkling: "In my heart of hearts God is closer to me than I am to myself."

At the same time, St. Augustine knows also the other half of our heart's paradox: "Restless is our heart until it finds rest in you, God." The tension between most intimate belonging and most ardent longing keeps our heartstrings in tune. From hive to blooming meadow and back home our hearts keep winging their way; from the invisible through the visible and then — heavy with harvest like bees with baggy pants of pollen and bellies bulging with nectar — back home to "the great golden honey-comb of the invisible." This is the pattern of our

23

heart's repeated journeys throughout life and of life's quest as a whole.

In one of his *Poems for the Hours of Prayer* Rilke describes the beginning of our life's journey in a kind of miniature creation myth. This myth is so relevant to our task of making sense of the senses that I will paraphrase it here: God, in creating humans, speaks to each one of us personally, but only before we are completely fashioned; after that, God goes with us out into the darkness and is silent. The Creator's words which we dimly hear, before we are led out into the night, are these: "Urged on by your senses, go forth to the very brink of your longing. Clothe me, the Invisible, in what is visible!" (But how can this be done?) "Grow like a fire behind all things so that their expanding shadows keep covering all of me. Let everything happen to you: beauty and terror. Keep going, no matter what. No sensation is too far out. Let nothing separate you from me." (And then, the Creator's parting word:) "The land which they call 'life' is near. You will recognize it by its serious demands. Give me your hand!"

Who says there are no longer myth-makers among us? Doesn't this contemporary myth pluck deep archetypal chords within us? Urged on by our senses we sail to the farthest shores of our longing. But what is this longing if not homesickness? We long for belonging, for home; yet, home was our very starting point. We find this pattern in many myths and fairy tales: the hero journeys through lands and seas in search of a longed-for treasure and finds that treasure at last back in the very place where the quest began.

Does this not ring true to your own experience? Longing drives us on and on. But if we let everything happen to us — terror no less than beauty — and keep going, we may hope to arrive and find ourselves at last at that firm center which we never left. "Home is where one starts from," says T. S. Eliot in his *Four Quartets*.

> We shall not cease from exploration
> And the end of all our exploring
> Will be to arrive where we started
> And know the place for the first time. (IV:V)

The voyage to the brink of our longing is a home-coming to our heart of hearts. Here in our heart alone the divine fountain of meaning wells up. As we drink from it, all that our senses have brought home from the long journey makes sense at last. For, nothing makes sense until we learn to listen with our heart.

We have said that the heart, where self and all and God are united, is the crossroads of the visible and the invisible. For this reason the heart is also our organ for meaning. Our eyes see, but only our heart looks through things to their meaning. Our nose registers scents, but only our heart will track like a hound its ethereal quarry. Our tongue tastes, but only a heart can feast. Skin touches skin, but being in touch is a matter of the heart. Our ears hear, but only a listening heart understands.

This brings us to the decisive question: How can we learn to listen with our *heart?* How shall we go about it? My own experience suggests that this process of learning to find sense through one's senses resembles a three-step dance. The three steps I have in mind might be called Childlike Openness, Youthful Courage, and Mature Communion.

What I am calling Childlike Openness is an attitude with which every one of us was born. Babies are quite naturally open and trusting in every way; the tingling readiness of all our senses is simply part of this. When we lose this spontaneity we can regain it only with difficulty. But losing it is inevitable. One reason may be that our trusting openness gets betrayed and we "clam up." But even without any hurt, freshness and excitement wear off; as time goes on, the excitement subsides, and our senses are no longer wide open for whatever comes along.

Children themselves seem to be dimly aware that things get a bit dull once they become used to them. In the villages of Tibet, on the islands of the Pacific, in the outback of Australia, in our own country, and everywhere else in the world, children invent and re-invent the following game: You join thumb and forefinger to form a peep-hole and look through; the whole world looks suddenly new and surprising.

Toy stores sell a kind of kaleidoscope that differs from the old ones that let you see chips of colored glass as marvellous stars by reflecting them in mirrors inside a tube. These new ones allow you to point the tube like a telescope at any object you choose and turn it into a star. Things to which you never gave a second look suddenly thrill you, when you see them in a new way.

You can get this thrill less expensively: just push the point of a pencil through a sheet of paper and use this hole for a minute as your window on the world. Surprise! My own hand becomes a whole landscape of unsuspected vistas. Since I no longer get the whole hand into view at once, not even a whole finger, I cannot get away with simply checking off concepts like "hand" or "finger" without another glance. And when I do look, what I see is not as slick and abstract as those concepts in my mind. What on earth are these bulging, brown folds like out-of-shape bellows of a minute accordion? A split-second before the word "knuckles" flashes through my mind, I have for once really looked.

This kind of looking can be learned. We can train ourselves in it. And this training will be fun, as soon as the child in us wakes up and begins to play. Nothing could be more important for our well-being on all levels than this awakening. Only our Inner Child can tingle with delight at simple pleasures like bare feet in wet grass, a slide into a swimming pool, or the smells of a picnic. We need to find that child hiding inside

The path to God starts at the gates of perception. But they often creak on rusty hinges.

us, let it out, let it run about without clothes, let it have fun. In no other way can we recover the joy of all our senses. But this recovery is nothing less than the first step towards finding meaning in life. *"How should tasting touching hearing seeing breathing ... doubt unimaginable YOU?"* asks e.e. cummings. The child in us spontaneously makes a beeline to the Source of Meaning and sips sweetness with all its senses. The path to God starts at the gates of perception.

Most people's glorious gates of perception creak on rusty hinges. How much of the splendor of life is wasted on us because we plod along half-blind, half-deaf, with all our senses throttled, and numbed by habituation.

27

How much joy is lost on us. How many surprises we miss. It is as if Easter eggs had been hidden under every bush and we were too lazy to look for them. But it need not be so. We are able to stop the advance of dullness like the spread of a disease. We can even reverse the process and initiate healing. We can deliberately pay attention each day to one smell, one sound which we never appreciated before, to one color or shape, one texture, one taste to which we never before paid attention. Try for just one week to dedicate each day to cultivating a different one of your senses. Monday: smell day; Tuesday: taste day; and so on. Since there are two more days in a week than the acknowledged five senses, I suggest you give three days to the much neglected sense of touch.

We long to be in touch with life, to touch and to be touched. Yet, we are also afraid of letting anything "get at us." Afraid of letting life come too close, we keep it at arm's length and don't even realize what fools we are making of ourselves. We are going through life like someone stepping into the shower, carefully keeping the umbrella up. We are holding on to our hats, our tokens of social identity and respectability. Far be it from us to make fools of ourselves! It takes a bit of life experience to realize that our choice is merely between making fools of ourselves either intentionally or unintentionally. By refusing to dare and make fools of ourselves willingly and wisely, we make fools of ourselves foolishly.

Noelle Oxenhandler, whose poems deserve to be more widely known, speaks with the wisdom of a woman willing to make a fool of herself. Her poem *Woods* is so relevant to our concerns in this chapter that I will quote it in full:

I wish to grow dumber,
to slip deep into woods that grow blinder
with each step I take,
til the fingers let go of their numbers
and the hands are finally ignorant as paws.
Unable to count the petals,
I will not know who loves me,
who loves me not.
Nothing to remember,
nothing to forgive,
I will stumble into the juice of berry, the
shag of bark,
I will be dense and happy as fur.

"Fur" — what a word with which to end a poem. Say it out loud and it will make you feel what "dense and happy" means. We cannot touch this dense happiness "til the fingers let go of their numbers." People who are stuck in numbers and other abstractions will never be in touch with life. Most of us are in no danger of missing the forest for the trees. It wouldn't hurt us to let go of abstractions like "forest" for a while and re-discover trees and "the shag of bark." The child in us — knees stained by the juice of berry, hair tangled with twigs and spider webs — can come out of hiding, this very day, and make us "dense and happy as fur."

This happiness lives right next door to joy. Joy goes beyond happiness. Joy is the happiness that does not depend on what happens. It springs from gratefulness. When we begin to take things for granted, we get sucked into boredom. Boredom is deadly. Yet, everything within us longs for "life, life in fullness" (Jn. 10:10). The key to life in fullness is gratefulness.

Sacred Sensuousness

Try this: Before you open your eyes in the morning, stop and think. Remember that there are millions of blind people in this world. Surely, you will open your eyes more gratefully, even if you'd rather keep them closed a little longer and snooze on. As soon as we stop taking our eyesight for granted, gifts spring into our eyes which we did not even recognize as gifts before. To recognize a gift as gift is the first step towards gratefulness. Since gratefulness is the key to joy, we hold the key to joy, the key to what we most desire, in our own hands.

Denise Levertov is so powerful a poet because she knows how to turn the key of gratefulness even during morning rush-hour traffic:

> Each day's terror
> almost a form of boredom—madmen
> at the wheel and
> stepping on the gas and
> the brakes no good —
> and each day one,
>
> sometimes two, morning-glories,
> faultless, blue, blue sometimes
> flecked with magenta, each
> lit from within with
> the first sunlight.

This "first sunlight" is not the first light of this day only, but of all days; it is the first light of the first day ever. And it is more: it is the "Light Invisible," the source of all visible light. The Psalmist sings to God, "By your light we see light" (Ps. 36:9) and this is why T. S. Eliot can write:

Sacred Sensuousness

We see the light but see not whence it comes.
O light Invisible, we glorify thee!
                                    Chorus X: from *The Rock*

Once we open our eyes, we cannot limit how far and how deep our sight will reach. We may compare the inner gesture of opening our eyes in this sense to jumping off a cliff. You will not stop falling after four feet because that is all you bargained for. At this point it becomes clear that our first step, Childlike Openness, sooner or later demands a second one: Youthful Courage.

Have you ever wondered why so many children seem bright, beautiful, and full of promise and so many grownups dull, humdrum, and stuck? Are these adults really the children of two decades ago? Will these wonderful youngsters turn into what their elders are now? "God forbid!" we sigh spontaneously. Generation after generation keeps longing that "a child shall lead them" (Is. 11:6) into a Peaceable Kingdom, a true homeland of the heart. This child is within each of us and will indeed lead us, if only we are willing to pay the price. That price is high: trust in life, come what may.

Every time we practice true openness of our senses, we exercise trust in life. Only if we have a trusting attitude can we open ourselves to the unfamiliar, the strange, the other. I remember the flash of insight that showed me why childlike openness demands so much courage and trust. I was talking with a group of students about the gushing source of energy which the world provides if we learn to drink it in with all our senses. At this point a woman in the group startled me with a question. "Why," she asked, "if all this is so delightful — and I know it is —

31

do I still feel some inner resistance to opening myself to such joy?" Before I could think of an answer, another student offered it: "I know where this resistance comes from in my own case: whenever I open myself to something beautiful, something else slips in and starts making demands on me."

How true! Rilke captures that moment when "something else slips in and starts making demands," in one of his best known sonnets, *Archaic Torso of Apollo.* In twelve masterly lines the poet draws us into the magic circle of a Greek sculpture, until we stand spellbound before this torso of glistening marble and are all eyes. At this instant, half-way into the next-to-last line of the poem, comes the turning point: suddenly we are aware that what we are looking at is looking at us. Abruptly the last line leaps at us: "There is not one spot" (on this marble surface) "that does not look at you." And the poem ends with the curt demand which the piercing look of reality makes on us: "You must change your life."

> **Poetic truth both dares us and inspires us to dare. Beauty blazes where eyes face truth fearlessly.**

Though I have read this sonnet countless times, still, at every new reading of it these lines come as a shock. What gives them so powerful an impact is that they ring so true, so universally true. Whenever we open our senses to beauty we lay ourselves open also to the demands of truth, for truth and beauty are one. Thus, we find ourselves challenged. Simply by its presence genuine goodness challenges the best in us. It needs no word, no raised index finger. It need not even be human goodness that confronts us in this way. Think of a brave, patient, faithful dog or horse. If you ever knew one, did it not make you feel both challenged and inspired? I have often thought: if only I could be as genuine as this four-footed friend. Since goodness and beauty are one, it takes courage to be open for beauty. Whenever beauty thrills us, goodness dares us.

Do children realize how much courage it takes to be open and trusting? They do not reflect on it, but they do realize it by acting. Only so can they grow. For it is only courage that makes us grow in strength as we rise to each new challenge, like horses made to jump higher and higher hurdles.

Cowards cease to grow. If we dare, we can continue to grow even now as we did when we were children, but now we can't help reflecting on how much courage this costs us. We will have to let go of our armor, of the iron bands around our hearts by which we hope to make ourselves invulnerable, succeeding only in becoming insensitive. You will start growing again in the measure in which you expose your heart to life — unshielded, vulnerable, but fully alive. The poet in us dares to live that way. Rilke characterizes this stance as that of rock climbers "exposed on the mountains of the heart."

Mountain climbing demands training. If we want to be fit for exposure "on the mountains of the heart" we shall have to train for it. Maybe a change of mental diet will help; maybe some nutritious supplements, like a poem a day. Not every poem speaks of that exposure of the heart explicitly, but implicitly every good poem does. It will put a spell on us and guide us to the point where beauty flares up and, with it, the burning challenge of goodness. A preachy poem never has that power. The raised index finger of a teacher breaks that spell. But the sound of truth — and this is what a good poem allows us to hear — the ring of truth will both dare us and inspire us with daring.

To inspire courage is one of poetry's priceless gifts. Yet, we rarely pay attention to this well-hidden effect of poems. We hardly become aware of their moral force, because it is so far removed from any moralizing. Instead, a great poem leads us to the very starting point of moral goodness: trust in life. And how persuasively it does so. In its truthfulness it simply shows us reality as both beautiful and good. How pedagogically wise true poets are, and this without any thought or intention of being didactic. Who can look deeply into the chalice of that morning glory "lit from within with/the first sunlight" and not yield to its wordless invitation? Will you go back to your "day's terror" unchanged? Or will the stillness you felt when its "faultless blue" ever so lightly brushed against you change your life just a little, making you more quiet, more centered, that day?

Good poems show us all things as they are and so give us courage to trust life even when it doesn't feel good. Yes, there are poems on daffodils, starlit nights, first love. But others that quickly come to mind deal with the pain of parting, with being lost, with grieving, shipwreck, or death. The truthfulness with which poets treat painful experiences unflinchingly lets beauty shine through. Courage in facing reality is contagious. Thus, our own trust in life begins to grow as if by osmosis.

Do you remember how we pored over adventure stories as adolescents? What enchanted hours we spent alone with a book in a favorite hiding place! Mine was way up in the branches of a walnut tree. We certainly did not read for the explicit purpose of character improvement. Ridiculous idea! We read for the sheer excitement of sharing our heroes' adventures. Yet, sooner or later, life challenged us to act as bravely as our heroes had done in those stories. Then, with some luck, we found that their example had made us ready for it.

With poetry it is not all that different. No one reads poems in search of moral improvement; it is the sheer delight in beauty that draws us. Beauty blazes whenever eyes face truth fearlessly. Thus, quite unawares we get accustomed to this way of looking, prepared to face the demands of real life with the same unflinching courage.

There are many methods for training one's courage. Reading poetry is not the most widespread one. We must find the method that suits us best. Whatever method we employ, youthful courage to face all aspects of reality with trust in life is the attitude we need to learn in our Step Two.

With this attitude we dare to go, in the words of Rilke's creation myth, "to the very edge of our longing." There we encounter something which goes beyond the senses. We reach the point where our being "all eyes" suddenly switches to an awareness of being looked at by a thousand eyes. If at that brink of "beauty and terror" we dare to let everything happen to us, we become aware of the challenge: "You must change your life!" What this change implies belongs to our discussion of Step Three.

The key word of our first step was "openness"; for the second step it was "courage"; this third step now concerns "transformation."

Sacred Sensuousness

Who does not know what T. S. Eliot means when he speaks of "music heard so deeply/that it is not heard at all, but you are the music/while the music lasts" *(Four Quartets;* III:V:210-212). Here we have a hint of "transformation." This example appeals to our sense of hearing. In the poem *Woods* we came across a different hint, one appealing to our sense of touch: As soon as "the fingers let go of their numbers" we became "dense and happy as fur." Through any one of our senses we can approach transformation. Approach, I say deliberately, for that is all we can do. We need to cultivate openness and practice courage; this is our task. But transformation, when it happens, is pure gift.

In discussing this third of our three steps towards making sense of the world through the senses we will need to stress three points. One: transformation is not an achievement, but pure gift. Two: it is not merely an aesthetic experience, but an existential one. Three: we are not being transformed into something else, but into our own true self.

Before we look at these points one by one, I must remind you again: do not take my word for any of this. Search your own awareness and rely on that. Nothing else will ever convince you. All I can do is encourage you to be attentive to aspects of our experience which we easily overlook. Our culture does not prepare us for being alert to refined sense impressions, let alone for following them when they lead us beyond themselves. For most people it would seem like complete nonsense to look at a sculpture until it "looks back from every point of its surface." Watch out before you tell just anyone that a Greek statue of Apollo gave you the message, *"You* must change your life!"

Our first point regarding transformation through sense experience will easily be granted. If you know from experience how it feels to listen to music so deeply that suddenly you are no longer over against the music as listener, but "you are the music/while the music lasts," then you know also that this is not your accomplishment, but an overwhelming gift. If, as a child, you had a Saint Bernard dog in whose shaggy coat you could dig your fingers and bury your face until you

The three steps of a listening heart:
1. Childlike Openness;
2. Youthful Courage;
3. Mature Communion.

became "dense and happy as fur," or if you have ever raised your eyes to snowy peaks reaching into a deep blue sky and felt everything within you rise and shine, then you know that these are moments of grace, nothing anyone could earn or deserve, but gifts, freely given.

Our second point may be less obvious. It claims an existential, rather than an aesthetic impact for moments when "you are the music/while the music lasts." If this impact were merely aesthetic, only our sense of beauty would be affected, but such moments are apt to affect our whole life. Peak experiences of this kind do not just tell us something about our taste. They show us who we are.

See if you can validate this claim against your own experience. Music is not the only realm in which sensual pleasure can reach so high a degree that it ignites, and in the blast makes our awareness fuse with its object. To many people this happens in nature or in sports —

think of marathon runners — or in art forms other than music.

We might ask: What kind of music is likely to be "heard so deeply/that it is not heard at all, but you are the music/while the music lasts"? Is this likely to happen with Muzak? To be heard so deeply music demands more than that we turn it on as we turn on a fan on a hot day. It demands that we truly listen, that we pay attention — *attention plus*. The "plus" consists in this: We must somehow give ourselves to music before it takes hold of us. Our laziness feels more comfortable with music for easy consumption than with music that is demanding. Demanding? Let us take this expression seriously. What does it imply?

Demanding and difficult are closely related terms, but there is a fine distinction between the two. Exploring what distinguishes the merely difficult from the demanding will help us find that edge of our awareness where the aesthetic plunges down into existential depth. As close as difficult and demanding are to each other, the difficult is not always demanding, nor is the demanding always difficult. Check some examples: You spilled coffee on your friend's newly upholstered couch; removing the stain may be difficult, though not demanding; admitting your clumsiness is demanding, but where is the difficulty? Climbing Annapurna may be unimaginably difficult and demanding yet, bowing to weather conditions and turning back a hundred feet below the summit is still more demanding, although it cuts short the difficulties.

Analyzing a piece of music according to all the intricacies of musicology is certainly more difficult than simply to sit back and listen with wholehearted enjoyment;

yet, to listen deeply is more demanding than to analyze the structure. Analyzing takes knowledge and skill; true listening takes all of you. It might not seem difficult to give ourselves to the rapture of beauty. Yet, out of it emerges a Presence, a Voice, name it as you wish, that goes beyond aesthetics and makes existential demands: "You must change. ..."

So far, I have made two points concerning this change: the transformation is not achieved but given, and it is not aesthetic but existential. My third point is that we are not transformed into something other, but into our own true self. It is this third point we must consider now. It will be helpful to start

> *Transformation:*
> *is gift,*
> *not achievement;*
> *is existential,*
> *not aesthetic;*
> *is self-fulfilment,*
> *not exchange of self.*

with an insight which Oscar Cullmann expressed when he wrote, "There is faithfulness at the heart of all things." The moment we stop taking for granted this faithfulness at the heart of things, we wake up. We find ourselves "at the brink of our longing." On this side is the multifarious fullness accessible to our senses; beyond is the simple fullness of its sense and meaning: the heart of all is faithfulness.

Instinctively we must have sensed this from the start. We could not have taken the first step, the first breath, had we not trusted that the world is trustworthy. A spark of trust glimmers in our guts. When we let it shine also in our heads and hearts, it becomes more than blind instinct; it becomes trust in life, trust in the very source of life; it becomes full-fledged faith, the only appropriate response to the faithfulness at the heart of all there is.

Is this the same as faith in God? Neither "yes" nor "no" is an adequate answer to this question. If I say "no," I am denying that trust in life is of one piece with trust in the source of life, called God. But if I say "yes," I am causing a short-circuit, since much of what passes as faith in God is merely a fearful clutching of beliefs and has little to do with its genuine counterpart. Genuine faith is courageous trust in God's trustworthiness.

This understanding of faith stands behind St. Paul's central claim: the message of Christ establishes the right relationship between God and humans "from faith to faith" (Rom. 1:17). This key formula traces the bond between God and us humans most succinctly "from (God's keeping) faith to (us having) faith" in God's reliability. In the biblical tradition human faith is the response to divine faithfulness. What we are talking about is not restricted, however, to any particular tradition or creed. It is a universal phenomenon accessible to every human heart. All who follow their senses to the faithful heart of reality find themselves both challenged and encouraged to a faith which all the creeds in the world presuppose as their common matrix.

Buddhist faith lets itself silently down into ultimate faithfulness. Hindu faith meets that faithfulness in the cave of each one's own heart. Biblical faith expresses the encounter with faithfulness in terms of dialogue, "God speaks."

The Bible conceives of everything as created by God's word, and so as actually being a word. In this world view every thing, every person, every situation is at its core a spelling out of God's faithfulness calling for a response of faith on the hearer's part. Do not deny too quickly that you know what is meant by the poetic image, "God speaks." Yet, don't take my word for it either. Search your own awareness. We are talking about something that is easily missed, "a small, still voice," easily drowned out by our own noises, something shy that wants to be befriended. Only when we become ever so quiet inside do we sense in the smallest speck of reality a great Presence, both strange and familiar, waiting to meet us. Strange this Presence seems to us, because it differs from all else we know; at the same time, we seem to know it more intimately than anything else we ever knew. We dread its strangeness; we long for its intimacy. It is this Presence that looks at us, when we dare to expose ourselves "on the heart's mountains" and demands our transformation: "You must change. ..."

To speak of a Presence is a somewhat poetic way of personification; yet we have no other way to express so subtle an aspect of reality. Let us remember, though, that we are exploring reality, not a fiction of our imagination. On one level we are saying nothing more profound than that a boulder will faithfully remain rock; that a goat will remain a goat through and through; that an oak tree will display oakness to the core, and hydrogen will reliably be itself down to a single atom. What catapults our awareness to a higher level is our capacity for surprise.

If you have never been surprised that your dog remains so dependably a dog and does not turn suddenly into a kangaroo or a hippopotamus, chances are that you are still taking reality a bit too unquestioningly for granted. Allowing ourselves to be surprised that things are what they are makes us wake up as from a deep sleep. Children, before we clip the wings of their adventurous minds, are capable of this kind of surprise in which Plato recognized the root of all philosophy. It can be cultivated. Cultivating surprise will do wonders for our wakefulness, our aliveness.

Wakeful attention makes us aware of facts we had overlooked in a more superficial contact with reality; the fact, for instance, that in a real sense we become that to which we give ourselves with all our senses. Remember T. S. Eliot's experience of becoming music; remember what it does to you when you watch skaters dancing weightlessly as it seems on a mirror of ice. An orchard in bloom makes us bloom inside. Beauty seen makes the one who sees it more beautiful. The Presence transforms us into itself: Reality makes us real. Here we have reached a decisive insight: to the extent to which we respond with faith to the faithfulness at the heart of reality we ourselves become real.

All the toy animals in the children's story *The Velveteen Rabbit* have one great longing: to become real. Discussing this, while the children are sleeping, the Teddy bears ask the wise, old rocking horse, "Does it hurt to become real?" The answer is, "When you become real, you no longer mind the hurt." The deepest reason for our refusal to wake up and to respond fully to reality is our timid flinching in the face of its hardness. In the measure in which we brave the hurt we become real.

This transformation is pure gift, is existential, and — as my third contention claimed — transforms us not into something other, but into ourselves. Becoming real is transformation into our own true self. Here, once again, Rilke finds the perfect expression. In his poem *A Walk* he speaks of "that which we cannot grasp" — the Presence — as grasping us and transforming us "into that which unawares we are." It cannot be put more succinctly. What we experience as a Presence is the trustworthiness of that which is ultimately real. Through courageous trust in this ultimate reality we become real, i.e., we realize our being one with it.

But does this formula remain valid also if those who feel comfortable enough with the word "God" use it in place of ultimate reality? It ought to work, for it would be a sorry God who was not ultimately real. Can we say, then, that by opening our senses wide and courageously to reality we can reach that ultimate goal of our longing, God in us, our own true self? Yes, indeed. By this affirmation we merely reaffirm what St. Augustine knew: Our heart is restless in its quest until it finds God who is from the start closer to us than we are to ourselves, who is the true Self of ourselves.

Consider the remarkable implications. We can indeed find sense through our senses; even ultimate sense, ultimate meaning. Full acceptance of our sensuousness is a genuine spiritual path. Even for spiritually aware Christians the discovery of sacred sensuousness at the core of their own tradition can come as a startling surprise.

Discovering sacred sensuousness is like waking up from a stupor into which Christian spirituality fell in spite of itself, long ago. This awakening is the beginning of a genuinely incarnational spirituality. Sacred sensuousness takes it seriously that God is not only beyond all that we can imagine, but is also the very source of the sensuous reality that feeds our imagination. What a privilege for us to be alive in this period of history when more and more people are waking up to the realization that sensuousness is sacred. Not as if this were some new fangled fad. It is merely a re-discovery of the healthy biblical enjoyment of the senses in which Jesus himself was brought up and felt at home. In that same spirit, Irenaeus, one of the earliest Christian theologians, coined the famous saying, "The glory of God is the human being fully alive." Surely this implies aliveness of all the senses. Irenaeus continues, "Life for humans is to see God." How could we expect to see God if we are insensitive to God's Self-revelation to us through all our senses?

St. Benedict urges us to open our eyes to the *Deificum lumen* — the light that makes the beholder divine. This is one of the boldest expressions in Christian spiritual literature. And it stands not in some obscure passage but in a document that has inspired the Christian tradition for three quarters of its history. One has to go to the Latin original in order to get the full impact of St. Benedict's words. Translations turn strangely bland if not outright evasive when they reach this passage, too timid to face "the light that makes divine." Admittedly we are dealing with a bold expression here, but nothing short of such boldness can do justice to the bold Good News of transformation "from faith to faith."

Re-discovering sensuousness as sacred is re-discovering Incarnation Spirituality at the heart of Christianity.

Our waking up to sacred sensuousness is only the beginning of transformation, the beginning of a life-long adventure. Opening one's eyes to "the light that makes divine" is only the first step of "walking in the light"

(1 Jn. 1:7). Personal transformation is only the starting point for a transformation of the whole world by those to whom the thunder voice calls out, "You are the light of the world" (Mt. 5:14). We shall take a closer look at this challenge in the next chapter. What we have established here, I hope, is that in a spirituality faithful to Jesus Christ sensuousness is not suspect but sacred. A listening heart recognizes in the throbbing of reality pulsating against all our senses the heartbeat of divine life at the core of all that is real.

Sensuous Asceticism

No matter how high it flies, sooner or later, spirituality has to come down to earth. The point of touchdown is asceticism. This is the reason why asceticism is an element of every spiritual tradition, an indispensable element of all spiritual training. Genuine spiritual practice will inevitably include training of the body, since after all we are not disembodied beings. The method by which the body is made transparent for the light of the spirit and aglow with its fire is asceticism.

I look up synonyms for asceticism and am appalled: abnegation, penance, mortification, nothing but negative terms. I skip to the noun "ascetic"; here the list of synonyms culminates in "self-tormentor." The notion of asceticism has been twisted out of shape by an unhealthy attitude towards the body. In contrast I remember gratefully the body image with which I grew up. A ditty I liked as a child sums up the appreciation of the body that was instilled in me; roughly translated it reads:

> A crystal is your soul.
> It shines with light divine.
> For this most treasured gift
> Your body is the shrine.

On Sunday afternoon visits to the Hapsburg treasure chamber in Vienna, my brothers and I had stared in wonder at treasure chests gilded and jewel-studded even on the outside. They shaped my idea of the body as a shrine of the soul and of the reverent treatment my body deserved. This shaped my own view of asceticism.

The word "ascetic" comes to us from the sports vocabulary of ancient Greece. Originally it referred to the workout by which athletes kept themselves in good shape. Only much later was the same word used by those aspiring to become "spiritual athletes" through special exercises. Readers of the New Testament are familiar with sports metaphors: training, competing, playing by the rules, sprinting, boxing, winning a trophy. St. Paul used these images in his letters and later Christian writers followed his model. Asceticism is methodical effort towards spiritual progress. But what is spiritual progress?

Since "spirit" means "life breath" and spirituality is aliveness on all levels, spiritual progress must be measured not only by increasing mental awakeness, but also by bringing the body's spirited vigor up a few notches. The summary of Jesus' aspiration, his mission statement as it were, "that they may have life, life in abundance" (Jn. 10:10) would be a bit ridiculous if this "abundance" did not include the body. This provides the basis for Sacred Sensuousness and also for an asceticism that trusts the senses rather than holding them suspect. In spite of past and present deviations from its innate impetus, Christian asceticism is by its very nature sensuous asceticism.

The key word for methodic training in spirituality is gratefulness. The word explains itself: gratefulness is the full response to what is *gratis,* freely given, pure grace.

Sensuous Asceticism

The given is always at hand, in any given situation in this given world; fullness of response to this gift is the goal; what needs to be improved by practice is our response. It may be a good idea to start with some simple exercise. Why not start spiritual training with a foot bath? For an experience in which our senses spontaneously spark off a grateful response, a foot-bath is not a bad choice. Your heart and your tongue may not yet be ready, but in their own way your toes will start to sing gratefully. Can anyone deny that this is a step in the direction of "life abundant"?

Day and night gifts keep pelting down on us. If we were aware of this, gratefulness would overwhelm us. But we go through life in a daze. A power failure makes us aware of what a gift electricity is; a sprained ankle lets us appreciate walking as a gift, a sleepless night, sleep. How much we are missing in life by noticing gifts only when we are suddenly deprived of them! But this can be changed. We need some methodical exercise in gratefulness. Years ago, I devised a method for myself which has proved quite helpful. Every night I note in a pocket calendar one thing for which I have never before been consciously thankful. Do you think it is difficult to find a new reason for gratitude every day? Not just one, but three and four and five pop into my mind, some evenings. It is hard to imagine how long I would have to live to exhaust the supply.

As our alertness improves with practice, we notice that it is actually the same gift we receive under countless different appearances; this gift is opportunity. Opportunity is the gift for which all other gifts are merely packaging. And more surprising still: out of 100 opportunities, 99 are opportunities to enjoy — enjoy what we receive. That this surprises us is in itself a measure of our lack of attentiveness. On difficult days, we have eyes only for our difficulties; on easy days we seem to have no eyes at all. Ungratefully we tend to take whatever good comes our way for granted and balk at the rest. Thus we miss innumerable opportunities for grateful joy.

We need to set up reminders. Thich Nhat Hanh, a Vietnamese monk and great spiritual teacher, rings what he calls a Mindfulness Bell at his monastery, many times throughout the day. Two Sisters of Mercy I used to know had their own mindfulness bell. Every time the grandfather clock in their old house struck the hour or the half-hour, the two became messengers of mindfulness for each other, like the angels after whom they were named. Sister Gabriel would say, "Remember God's presence!" waiting for Sister Michael's reply, "and be always grateful!" This may sound a bit eccentric, but in reality it was the very opposite: not a being out-of-the-center (ec-centric) but a centering in. Always in demand, caring for retarded children, befriending street people, serving the sick; the two Sisters called each other back to a great stillness at the center of their whizzing activities, to a Presence. Try it yourself and see what happens. Time turns from ticking into singing. *Chronos,* the impersonal time of chronometers, turns into personal *Kairos,* into grace-given opportunity. As *Kairos,* the Now becomes an opportunity to meet beyond all gifts the Giver.

Here I remember the formal installation of a Buddhist abbot. Chanting, candles, clouds of incense, gold brocade, chrysanthemums — a solemn ceremony in flawless ritual perfection. Suddenly the beeper on someone's wristwatch goes off. Deeply embarrassed, everyone identifies with the poor wretch to whom this happened.

Sensuous Asceticism

The newly ordained abbot's voice breaks the silence. "This was my beeper," he announces. "I have taken a vow to interrupt whatever I am doing, at twelve noon every day and to think thoughts of peace. Will you please join me in this, now, for a moment? Our world needs it."

Once we set out on the path of mindfulness, one step leads to the next. The opportunity which a given moment offers to us is almost always an opportunity to enjoy — 99 out of a 100 times. (This is so important that it bears repetition.) We need to test this claim by our own experience, for it provides the basis for the next step. Once out of a hundred times we will be challenged to respond fully and gratefully to something which we cannot enjoy. This, too, is given reality; it, too, is gift. Although I cannot enjoy it, will I still be grateful? It all depends on whether or not I have learned to unwrap the gift-within-the-gift: opportunity. The gift-wrapping may be enjoyable or not; opportunity — the real gift — is always opportunity to grow. If I avail myself of this opportunity, even though I do not enjoy the wrapping, I have made a decisive step forward. Those who make that step prove that they are serious about mindfulness, willing to follow that path all the way. Ascetic training begins with occasions which easily evoke a grateful response and prepares us for rising gratefully even to difficult occasions — to the opportunity (and challenge) of standing up for our convictions.

This shows a surprising connection between two poles held together in creative tension by sensuous asceticism: lively responsiveness to the pleasure of our senses is one pole, responsible social engagement is the other. What the two have in common is wakeful alertness for opportunity and grateful willingness to respond.

Alert responsiveness is the essence not only of gratefulness but also of obedience. Obedience? We do not normally pay attention to the fact that obedience and gratefulness are simply two faces of the same coin. Response is the key word that links the two. Both gratefulness and obedience are essentially response, the human heart's response to the heart of reality. When we realize that everything in this given world is gift, the heart's fitting response is gratefulness. And when we realize that through everything in life "God speaks" to us, the fitting, the wholehearted response is obedience.

Rightly understood, obedience does not consist in simply doing what one is told to do. Any properly trained poodle can do that. Obedience in the full sense is a mature human response: the heart's willing reply to the call of a given moment.

If our gratefulness is genuine it will be obedient; it will not depend on whether a wish of ours is fulfilled or denied. In obedient gratefulness we listen to reality more than to our wishful thinking; we keep our eyes on the Giver more than on the gift. In turn, if our obedience is genuine it will be grateful, not judging. Whether we hear a "yes" or a "no," we will obey willingly and cheerfully, grateful for the guidance we receive. A red light is as helpful in guiding traffic as a green one.

There is, however, an aspect of ascetic obedience — its most important one — which is missing in drivers' manuals: obedience listens to the Voice within the voices. This voice of reality "out there" is the same that speaks "within," as the voice of our own genuine self. Thus, obedience follows not some external command, but our heart's own deepest desire.

Sensuous Asceticism

To distinguish the genuine voice from distracting voices takes practice. Guidance comes to the obedient heart from the heart of reality itself, as we face it with trust and courage and wide open senses. A scene from C. S. Lewis' *Perelandra* charmingly illustrates this key insight of sensuous asceticism. Ransom, the hero of this space novel, has traveled from Earth to Perelandra, a Paradise-like planet. There we watch him walking through a grove and plucking a fruit from an unknown tree. Through Ransom's eyes we see the ripe fruit's glow and fresh flush; we feel its smooth skin, its plump shape heavy in his hand; with Ransom we smell its fragrance, taste its tart flesh as it first resists his teeth and then melts on his tongue — a deliciously sensuous experience. Ransom licks the juice from his chin and his fingers and — Earthling that he is — typically looks for more. Just as he reaches out, wanting to clutch the next fruit, something surprising happens: he hears — not with his ears, but nevertheless hears — this second fruit saying a loud and clear, "No. One was enough!"

In asceticism delight is primary. Renunciation is merely a means for more genuine delight.

This whimsical story is worth some attention. The setting is imaginary but the experience springs from sober perception; we can check it out by our own experience. This could correct a tendency to give first place to renunciation when we think of asceticism. No. Delight must come first. Had Ransom not opened all his senses to the "yes" of delight, he would not have heard the "no" of renunciation. And yet, too often ascetic practice is presented not as learning wholehearted attention, but as fitting into some mold of abstinence; not as joyful attunement of all our senses, but as their rejection. Thus, asceticism becomes "mortification" — literally "killing" — instead of life-affirming listening with a grateful heart.

This can lead to dreadful distortions. No wonder we find a healthy hesitation even among spiritually serious people, today, when the topic of asceticism comes up. We have been misled too often. A sound intuition tells us: delight deserves first place and renunciation itself is merely a means for greater, more genuine delight. Bernard of Clairvaux, an ascetic if there ever was one, listed the benefits of fasting. On top of this list he put: "food tastes so much more delicious when you are hungry." Eventually asceticism can take us far beyond sensuous pleasure, but unless it starts with the senses it will take us nowhere. Our senses are sparkplugs for healthy ascetical practice; the spark of joy starts it off; what keeps it running is obedience. Without obedience asceticism does not even deserve its name; it is simply debauchery upside-down. But with obedience, with loving listening we discover step by step new levels of joy. Gradually we begin to discern that sense, that meaning, to which the senses can only point the way.

To miss the transition from sensuous delight to a delight beyond the reach of our senses is to miss the upward movement of the inner life. Without the runway of the senses we could never take off. Yet, how shall we get airborne if we stick to the runway? In order to move through the senses to sense we must leave the senses behind.

Sensuous Asceticism

Long before the official expiration date of our life expectancy, we begin to notice a gradual diminishment of sensual keenness. If we don't want to get stuck in dead-end living we need to push through to "life-end" dying. The sooner we start, the better. Active dying is life affirming. Its secret of success: letting go. This gives us great inner freedom; freedom to ask: what is it time for now? Time to find what we have always been after, the joy at the core of pleasure, the joy that outlasts pleasure.

With his eyes on this lasting joy St. Paul writes to the Church at Corinth, a city famous for sensuous pleasure if not sensuality, "though outwardly we wear out, inwardly we grow stronger, day by day" (2 Col. 4:16). And St. Benedict promises to monks on the path of obedience, "which is bound to be narrow at the outset," that they will come to run and feel their "hearts expanding with unspeakable delight" (Prologue. 49). As one by one our senses let us down, obedience lifts us up. A listening heart can make sense even of the failing of our senses. It has ears for the challenge contained in this sagging; the challenge to rise above all that passes away. Because obedience guides the hearts of true ascetics, they taste all that the senses perceive of passing reality, find it good to the last drop, and still keep their hearts open for a reality beyond passing — for the faithful Presence at the core of all things, for ultimate meaning.

What our senses are after is sense. The goal of all our striving is meaning. Only in sense, in meaning, do our restless hearts come to rest. This end and aim of all our endeavors is also the goal of every ascetical practice. We need asceticism, because our senses do not automatically yield sense. When we deal with living reality, nothing is ever automatic. Life demands what no machine can give: courage. Unfolding life is an organic whole with death. To live means to die with every heartbeat and to be born anew, to breathe out with every breath what is old and to breathe in what is new. This demands courage: the courage to let go. Growing is dying into greater aliveness. This is true of growing old no less than it is of growing up. Both demand courage. Without courage we can neither live nor die. Courage to live is courage to die and courage to die is courage to live. We need that courage for our senses to die into sense.

This is the meaning of the motto, *Memento Mori,* which we find on ancient sundials — "Remember Dying": Remember that this is your task, not later on, once and for all, but here and now, again and again. To remember dying in this way is to come alive. Now and then, one of the sundials will read *Memento Vivere!* The message remains the same: "Remember Living!" Awareness of dying belongs to mindful living as the horizon belongs to the landscape. Death is the horizon of life's landscape; sense is the horizon of the landscape of the senses. The horizon lies always beyond; we

Blessing is the lifeblood throbbing through the universe. Sensuous Asceticism keeps it flowing.

can distinguish it from the landscape, but we cannot separate the two. The same is true of sense and the senses. Reject the senses, how will you find sense? Get stuck in the senses and life will be equally senseless. Both of these dead-end roads are laid out by human willfulness.

Sensuous Asceticism

Obedience, the opposite of willfulness, willingly follows the flow of life to its meaning: through the senses to sense.

Our most precise English word for the meaningful flow of life is "blessing." This may come as a surprise. Does not to bless mean making something holy by a religious rite, to sanctify, to invoke divine favor upon someone, to honor and glorify? Yes, but all these significations derive from one basic meaning: to strengthen the flow of the life force. The words blessing and blood go back to the same root. So do blossom, blade, bloom and other words that have to do with swelling life. Blessing is the spiritual lifeblood throbbing through the universe. "Praise God from whom all blessings flow," Christians sing, as they bless God. Blessing comes from God and flows back to its Source, just as blood comes from and returns to the heart. Sensuous asceticism may be understood as the practice by which we strengthen that flow of life. We open ourselves with all our senses to the goodness of life, let our hearts be filled to overflowing, and make that life-force flow out to all.

Blood is alive only as long as it keeps flowing. This is true also of blessing. An unforgettable image has imprinted this truth on my mind: the river Jordan flows down from Mount Hermon and becomes a natural symbol of blessing — life-giving water for parched soil. Nowhere is this blessing of water more striking than by the lake into which the Jordan flows from the north — Yam Kinneret, Lake Tiberias, the Sea of Galilee. Its shores are a paradise of orchards, fields, and gardens; its clear water is teeming with fish. From there the Jordan flows out again and meanders on southward toward another body of water, the Dead Sea. What contrast! Here the shores are a desert, the water a salty brine, unfit for irrigation, deadly for fish. The same water that feeds the Dead Sea feeds the lake that is the life of Galilee. But there it flows in and flows out again; the Dead Sea does not pass its water on. It remains, and stagnates. Blessing that stops flowing becomes a curse.

The truth that life and death make sense is not accessible to the senses. Nor is it something our intellect can prove. But our heart rises to this conviction when we give ourselves willingly to blessing received and blessing passed on. When all is said and done, only this makes sense: to be a channel of blessing. In the continuous flow of blessing our heart finds meaning and rest.

Let us look at practical examples. How can we learn to look and to listen, to smell, touch, and taste in a way that offers no resistance to the current of blessing? There are practices for making eye and ear, nose, skin, and tongue more effective sluices, channeling life-giving water into our hearts and from our hearts into a world in need of irrigation. We shall focus on them one by one, always beginning with sensuous delight and ending with some pointer towards implicit demands, thus holding together in creative tension the two poles of sensuous asceticism.

When the 23rd Psalm speaks of the banquet the Lord has spread out for us, this is a fitting image for the sensuous treats this world offers to every one of our senses. Before we give any further thought to ascetical practice let us make sure we have the right attitude towards this given world. Let us see it as what it is: a banquet for our senses. What can give more joy to the host than the joy of the guests? And how can we show our gratitude better than by digging in at this home-cooked meal? Children do that unabashedly. Only we grown-ups act as though we needed coaxing. Without a doubt the Heavenly Banquet will resemble a children's party far more than a formal dinner. Let's get ready *now*.

The Fulani in West Africa have a proverb that claims: "Eyes don't eat, but know what's good to eat." True, but we can also speak of "hungry eyes," of eyes that "devour" what they look at. Children in India are taught to eat their food first through their eyes, "like gods," before putting it into their mouths. This is worth trying for yourself. Why not make it a habit to look at your food for a few silent moments before "digging in"? Whole new dimensions of enjoyment are waiting for you to discover them.

> *Heaven's Banquet must resemble a children's party far more than a formal dinner.*

When we speak of "a feast for the eyes," this may refer to a tastefully laid-out buffet, but more often to some non-edible display, to flowerbeds or costumes of a ballet, to beauty that feeds our hearts through our eyes. In this sense, the whole visible world is a mouthwatering smorgasbord of sights that will even make our eyes water, for our hearts will overflow with grateful joy if only we look.

"Look at the stars! Look, look up at the skies! O look...!" G. M. Hopkins urges us breathlessly in the opening line of *The Starlit Night*. Yes, even by night there is more to be seen than the eye can hold. By day, we are simply overwhelmed. If you want to learn to look, start by night. What color is the night sky? Blue? What kind of blue? To call the color of the sky, of blueberries, larkspur, distant hills, of a sailor's cap, a bruise on your shin, and the eye of a peacock's feather simply "blue" is about as sophisticated as to say, "food," when the waiter comes to take your order in a French restaurant. And yet, what can we do? Our vocabulary is incredibly limited. To make up for this deficiency I like to stop at the paint department of our local hardware store and look at the color charts: Royal Blue, Turquoise, Navy, Plum, Steel, Huckleberry, Granite, Periwinkle, Thistle — not bad. Some brands wax poetic: Spa Blue, Frozen Sky, Azure Foam, Cool Eve, Neptune, Ice Cap. I have even found Lavender Twilight, Skier's Trail, Whispering Wind, Meditation, and — a most special blue — Nirvana.

Amidst all these riches our eyes stay hungry for more. Even the Bible assures us, "the eye is not satisfied with seeing" (Qo. 1:14) — no, never. This is so, because, as the Fox told the Little Prince: "It is only with the heart that one can see rightly; what is essential is invisible to the eye." And so, all human eyes stay ever hungry for what is essential — for meaning. Only our hearts can perceive meaning in (and beyond) what our eyes behold.

We tend to think of eyes as merely receiving light, but in a deeper sense eyes are also giving out light. One and the same thing will be different things as different eyes behold it in their own light. A bunch of rags can become a beloved baby doll in the light of a child's look. This light is as real as the light of a lamp — more real, in fact; real on a higher rung of meaning. You can feel its transforming power. Recall how a child's eyes looking into yours can fill you with brightness. Where blessing flows freely through the eyes into the heart, it flows generously out through radiant eyes.

Sensuous Asceticism

Everything depends on keeping blessing freely flowing. The clogging and choking of this flow is a constant hazard in an affluent environment. On my travels to different parts of the world I was astonished to find everywhere that it is the eyes of poor and simple people that shine. This bright luster is dimmed in direct proportion to an increase in possessions and complexities. Photographs in *National Geographic* bear this out.

Or look at snapshots of yourself as a child, a teenager, an adult, and you will notice how in your own eyes "the visionary gleam," as Wordsworth calls it, fades away as you forget the glories you have known. We forget the glorious freshness which met our childhood eyes; we forget to look for that same freshness today. It is still here, but a surfeit of impressions dulls our attention. The ascetical practice of mindfulness counteracts this process of deterioration.

Ascetical frugality is a sort of hydraulic management for the flow of blessing. The pressure of impressions rushes against our eyes more forcefully than against any of our other senses. Countless colors, shapes, and patterns are incessantly flashing before our eyes, each being swept out of view by the next before we have the leisure to look at it. No sooner is a visual seed sown than it is washed away from our flooded field of vision; there is no chance for us to reap "the harvest of a quiet eye." Not unless we make a wholehearted effort. Monks call this effort "custody of the eyes." This is an ascetical practice for which many, not only monks, feel an increasing need today.

By the time I first heard of custody of the eyes, this venerable practice had been whittled down to mere monastic etiquette. Thus, we American novices were relieved when Father Damasus told us with a laugh and a shrug, "Don't worry about custody of the eyes; that's a French virtue." But he also helped us recover its genuine meaning; he stressed that a novice has to learn everything anew: walking, breathing, and thus also looking. We came to find out through experience how right St. Benedict was in tracing haughty looks to a puffed up heart, and in telling monks that keeping one's eyes on the ground helps one to be humble, i.e., grounded.

Guarding our eyes means, above all, guarding them from overeating. "A well-trained child ought to be able to sit and look when nothing is to be seen," Native American wisdom tells us. Are children likely to learn this in front of their TV sets and computer screens? Yet, unless we learn it as children (or with greater difficulty later) our eyes will resemble gutters more than quiet pools that mirror the stars.

More and more consumers are becoming aware how important healthy nutrition is for our body. When will we begin to pay attention to how we nourish our mind? I know people who carefully count their calorie intake while stuffing their eyes and ears with a media diet of junk food. In our time, fasting must refer also to our media intake. What good is it to fast so that the life force will flow freely through the body and at the same time choke the mind by over-indulgence in visual intake? The goal of visual fasting is not to see less, but rather to look at less so as to see more. We need to cultivate healthy eating habits of the eyes.

We live in a time of visual inflation. For the price of a single meal anyone can buy a stunning reproduction of the *Book of Kells, Les trés riches heures du duc de Berry,* or Audubon's *Birds of America,* priceless books on which in former times only the most privileged ever laid eyes. A friend sent me a book with more than two thousand photographs of snowflakes, no two of them alike. To sit down with a picture book and not turn the page until you have looked at all there is to be seen can be as enjoyable now as it was when you sat on your mother's lap and did so. This exercise of sensuous asceticism can help restore to our eyes their "visionary gleam."

A closely related monastic practice is *lectio divina.* This "sacred reading" is not restricted to sacred texts. What makes it sacred is not *what,* but *how* we read. What matters is a quiet, unencumbered mind that allows blessing to rise from the page, "and through the eye correct the heart" (David Garrick, 1717–79). In fact, this kind of reading is not restricted to books. With the same attitude a monk will "read" the grain of wood in a piece of lumber and release the flow of blessing as he guides a plane. With this attitude we need also to read "the signs of the times" (Mt. 16:3).

The community in a House of Prayer invented a novel strategy for viewing the evening news on TV. When, after a section of news the commercials came on, all but one viewer would close their eyes and, with the sound turned off, hold prayerfully in their hearts what they had just seen. As soon as the person with open eyes turned on the sound again, the rest opened their eyes for the next news item. Although the difference between commercials and news is often merely the difference between advertisement and propaganda, this method was at least well-conceived. It was an effort to look with one's heart *through* the eyes, and not to take at face value what one sees *with* the eye. Blake's warning is still timely: It "leads you to believe a lie/when you look with, not through the eye."

When we learn to look *through* the eye, we will be able to "look through" in still another sense: to look through surface appearances to the heart of people and to the core of things and events. We will see what needs to be done. When we see signals for action, and — most important — respond, then and only then will blessing flow not only in through our eyes, but also out into the world.

This, too, was part of our eye training as novices. Some of us were always quick to see what needed to be done, like Martha in Luke's Gospel (Lk. 10: 38-42). And like Martha we tended to get annoyed at those who, like Mary in that story, "sat at the Lord's feet," reading or meditating, and couldn't be bothered. When we "Marthas" complained to Father Damasus, he would simply quote from the same page of the Gospel, "Blessed are the eyes that see what you see" (Lk. 10: 23): If you see what needs to be done, do it! Let blessing flow.

It has taken me more time and effort than I like to admit, but I have come to appreciate that piece of advice. We may not be able to do much when we see rainforests devastated, redwood forests secretly logged, chickens, calves, and pigs cruelly mistreated in factory farms, and other animals tortured in laboratories; when we see the rich getting richer and the poor poorer, money worshipped and human dignity sneered at. We may not be able to do much, but if we do the little we can do, our action will make a difference. It may not be more than the nibbling of a single mouse at the ropes that bind the world, but there are enough mice to make the thickest rope snap.

Sensuous Asceticism

If we muster the courage to look not with, but through our eyes, we shall find Yeats' word true in a twofold sense, "Everything we look upon is blessed" — blessed, as source of blessing when we look at it; blessed, because we look and act and so bring blessing to whatever we look at.

Our ears no less than our eyes can learn to channel blessing. All around us resounds an ocean of blessing that has its own tides. Both sound and silence are vital for our ears. Sounds we like and sounds we dislike carry a message. That message is more important than our likes and dislikes. We need to listen for it. Silence is essential for that listening. We need to cultivate silence.

Sounds we like are readily recognized as blessings. A morning in Hong Kong comes to my mind. I had spent the night with friends in a low-income apartment at Kowloon, an unimaginably overpopulated quarter of the city. In the first morning light I stepped out onto a small fourteenth-floor balcony. What flowed into my ears was not the traffic noise I had anticipated but, unaccountably at first, the warbling of innumerable song birds. High-rise apartment buildings blocked my view on every side, but on every balcony and windowsill I could see bird-cages. The little singers filled this 20th century concrete gorge with nature's ancient morning song "from sheer morning gladness at the brim" (Robert Frost, *The Tuft of Flowers*).

But what shall we do when traffic noise does batter our ears? Can we experience this, too, as blessing? One helpful habit I have learned is to refrain as long as possible from identifying unpleasant noises. As long as I manage to simply listen without giving a name to what I hear — "squealing brake" or "ambulance siren" — I am receiving a pure sense impression with no tag attached, no judgment made. Stripped of all labels, naked noises are at least worth my attention. In this noteworthiness lies a tiny seed of appreciation, a seed that might sprout and grow into a surprise.

In a House of Prayer I visited, the neighbor's bandsaw kept tormenting the people who had come there for a few days of silence. "How on earth can this screeching be a blessing?" one of them asked me, "It drives me up the wall!" My suggestion was, "try simply to listen; don't give the sound a name." In this case, it worked. A few days later, when I came back, I got this surprising account: "I did what you said, and when I forgot what it was, the noise suddenly sounded like the voice of an archangel." Although I can't claim to be an expert at distinguishing angelic voices, I feel that even

We may feel as weak as mice nibbling at the world's fetters. But we are many. The fetters must snap.

the voice of the lowest angel must be preferable to the shriek and whine of a bandsaw; it doesn't have to be an archangel's voice.

On second thought, is not everything we hear the voice of one angel or another? If "God speaks" and everything in creation spells out God's Word in its own unique way, and if angels are what their name means, "messengers," then everything audible deserves the attention due an angel's voice. The crackling of a campfire, summer rain drumming with small fingers on an umbrella, the long reverberation of a bronze gong — "appealing sounds" we call them. Half unaware of what we are saying, we acknowledge the appeal which the great message makes to our heart through sounds we call appealing. Appalling sounds, however, carry no less an appeal, a call, a demand, whether we like it or not. The biblical notion that "God speaks" through everything that exists leads with inner necessity to the exhortation, "Let those who have ears to hear, listen!" (Mt. 4:9).

How can we expect to hear in all things God's voice of silence, unless we stop producing a din that drowns out silence? Without silence there can be no listening. We need to renew our ancient friendship with silence; it is older than our flirtation with Muzak.

Primordial cultures still have ears for silence. Deep in the outback of Australia's Northern Territory I was privileged to be the guest of Aborigines who were still living in the bush like their ancestors, with no other shelter but the night sky and the comfort of five huge fires. Not far from their camp, the government had built a schoolhouse where their children were to be taught according to the same syllabus as city kids in Sydney or Perth. Their teachers, however, were Sisters of St. Joseph, women who had listening hearts and who became trusted friends of the tribal people. These wise women knew how to protect the inner silence of the children entrusted to them. In order to ease the culture shock they gathered their pupils not in the schoolhouse, but in the shade of a bough shed. In fact, they taught the children indirectly, through their mothers who came to school with them. Thus, they minimized alienation between the generations and fostered the traditional pattern for transmitting information. These teachers spoke softly, used images in preference to words, and gave their pupils much opportunity for non-verbal activities like drawing pictures. Still, school must have seemed like an avalanche of words to these children. At recess time between classes, they utterly surprised me. I was used to pupils bursting out into the schoolyard yelling and hollering. These children with their dark eyes, made darker still by their long eyelashes, walked out into the surrounding bush in complete silence, as if to wash their ears clean from too much talk.

The child within us, too, longs for silence. We must protect our children from injury through noise, a form of child abuse to which no one pays attention. A society must rid itself of causes for inner as well as for outer disease. Don't say this cannot be done. We have been able to ban smoking from public places, unthinkable though this seemed only a short time ago; we can do the same with Muzak. Smoking is no more damaging to lungs than Muzak is to hearts and minds. Little by little you can clean up noise pollution at least in your private environment. You can clear the channels of your heart's ear so that blessing can flow freely, once again.

Communication out of silence is true communication. All else is chitchat.

In Vienna, dear Sister Roswitha told her wide-eyed first graders that opening our mouth stretches the skin over our ears so that we can't hear well. Though I am not convinced concerning the anatomical details, the idea is correct. We have two ears and only one mouth; we ought to listen twice for every word we speak. Only communication that arises out of silence is true communication, the rest is chitchat.

Sensuous Asceticism

Once our heart is anchored in silence, we will be able to listen even while we are speaking. During one of the formal teaching sessions at Sonoma Mountain Zen Center, a sparrow started chirping outside. Stopping in mid-sentence, the Roshi put his palms together and bowed in silence, thanking for the bird's song. Not to be so wrapped up in our own talk that everything else becomes an annoying distraction — that takes practice.

Silence will make us hear appeals which noise drowns out: the sighs of devastated forests, the groans of lab monkeys with wired skulls, the sobs of mothers with babies at their emaciated breasts. We will begin to hear the truth that sets us free. As long as one creature in this world is oppressed and exploited, oppressor and victim alike lack freedom. Yet, "None so deaf as one who will not listen," as the proverb says. And in the year in which Hitler came to power, Samuel Butler wrote in his notebook: "Conscience is thoroughly well-bred and soon leaves off talking to those who do not wish to hear it." Yet, once we give our conscience permission to speak, we will hear words like, "Live simply, so that others may simply live!" As we begin to do this, blessing begins to flow. Then, the lifeblood of the world, so long clotted and encrusted, miraculously liquefies again, as is claimed for the blood of certain Saints. It will be a greater miracle still when we hear blessing pulsate again through the veins of the world.

Because of these implications for the whole world, sensuous asceticism is a serious matter — not dead serious, though, rather "life serious." Ascetical practice strives for increasing aliveness, and genuine life never lacks humor. Humor is a reliable litmus test for the authenticity of any spirituality.

Sensuous Asceticism

I have often wondered why there is something hu-
morous about our sense of smell. References to odors
are apt to trigger a snicker or an outright laugh. The reason may be that smell, more than any other sense, re-
leases childhood memories and makes our inner child
thumb his nose at the stilted etiquette of adults. In adult
company it is somehow not quite decorous to mention
smell, any smell, but above all body odor — pardon me,
I mean "B.O." We avoid even the word. "He smells best
that does of nothing smell." Is that so? I wonder if this
British proverb isn't an ironic reference to people whose
only virtue is that they are too blah to have vices. Day-
old babies have been found to recognize their mothers
by their smell. Who would want a mother "that does of
nothing smell," or a lover for that matter? Let's be hon-
est. Smells provoke a freeing laughter; "the truth will make
you free" — on this level, too. The child within laughs at
us, giggles at the ridiculous restraints of conventionality
to which we subject our native freedom.

If for nothing else, we deserve to be laughed at because our sense of smell is so underdeveloped. What
would your dog think of you if he suspected your pitiful
deficiency in this respect? Your prestige in dog circles
would be irreparably damaged.

The impoverishment of our language with regard to
smells reflects our neglect of this source of blessing. We
are surrounded by sage and chamomile and diapers and
salty sea breeze, by compost piles and aroma therapy
shops, by lavender soap, gasoline, herring barrels, bees-
wax, freshly-cut lawns, wood-smoke, and snow-wind, yet
we take all these gifts for granted. Familiar with horse
barns and dentists' offices, locker rooms, florist shops
and all the inexhaustible riches they offer to our noses,

most people know only two smells, "good" and "bad." So much potential pleasure goes to waste.

And what are "bad" smells, anyway? There are no bad colors in the spectrum, nor are there bad smells. I will admit only that smells sometimes occur in places where they don't belong. Even then, they remain interesting. To regain that interest for smells which we had as toddlers when we stuck our little noses into anything available, this alone would be a genuine spiritual accomplishment — the thrill of nearly dead senses rising to new life. When prophets in the Bible want to make fun of idols for being as dead as doornails, they jeer, "they have noses, but cannot smell!" (Ps. 115:6). Where the divine life-breath flows, noses come alive.

Mystics of all traditions find some of their most memorable metaphors in the realm of smelling. Kabir says that the bee of the heart stays deep inside the flower and cares for no other thing but for what he calls "the fragrance of 'I am He,'" or "the odor of the Holy One inside you." The penetrating quality of odors may account for the many passages in mystical literature in which fragrance becomes a metaphor for that all-pervading Spirit by which we know God. Of "the fragrance of that knowledge," Kabir says (again in Robert Bly's powerful translation): "It penetrates our thick bodies, /it goes through walls." And again: "the great doors remain closed, but the spring fragrance/comes inside anyway." We can hardly prevent this from happening. We can close our eyes and stop our ears, but how long can we hold our breath? As "the breath within our breath," the Divine Presence cannot be shut out.

"Delicious is the smell of your fragrance," whispers the bride in the Song of Songs to her divine lover, "your

Name is perfume poured out" (Sg. 1:3). And a New Testament passage picks up this thread of all-pervading presence when it turns the precious ointment poured out at Bethany into a symbol of the Good News. Where Mark speaks of the Gospel being preached "in the whole world," John says, "the whole house was filled with the fragrance of the perfume" (Mk. 14:9; Jn. 12:3). A multitude of mystical themes and poetic images ring through the passage of Jesus' anointing — in anticipation of his burial, as the story implies — especially the motif of Divine Wisdom who says of herself:

> I breathe forth a perfume like cinnamon and acacia,
> I exhale a fragrance like precious myrrh,
> Like galbanum resin, onycha, and balm,
> Like the smoke of incense in the Tabernacle.
>
> *Sir. 24:19ff*

Incense comes last in this passage. In contrast to the other scents mentioned, the fragrance of incense is set free only when the resin that contains it goes up in smoke and is, thus, sacrificed. The letter to the Ephesians (5:2) applies this to Jesus, seen as Divine Wisdom personified, giving his life as "an offering and a sacrifice to God for an odor of sweet fragrance." In the same sense Paul calls Christians "a sweet odor of Christ to God." Their lives are conceived as "spreading the fragrance of the knowledge of God in every place" — again the idea of the whole Earth house filled with the perfume of the Good News. Those who can't stand Christians find them "a deadly stench" (2 Co. 2:14-16). Using expressions like these, Paul surely wasn't alienated from his senses. His "incense" metaphor affirms what we said about the flow of blessing: when we fully open ourselves to blessing we become blessing. When we fully receive the fragrance of the Good News into our hearts, we ourselves become a fragrance of life for the life of the world.

Have you ever noticed that fragrance comes only in momentary wafts? We cannot hold on to it. We can look at the same color for hours, listen to the same tone for as long as we wish, but an odor must impinge on our nasal membranes in spurts in order to be perceived. The heavy honey smell of acacia or linden trees in bloom fills the evening air, but we perceive it only in wave after wave. Even if you dab cologne right into the hollow of your upper lip, you will smell it not continuously, but only in whiffs.

This points to another connection between smells and wisdom: we need to stay alert for moments of inspiration. The word "inspiration" means literally, "in-breathing." Only on an in-breath will we catch the scent that directs us like hounds that have a trained nose for where their duty lies. Like the senses of hounds our senses need to be trained so they will guide us from mere delight to delighted service. Wisdom proves its genuineness through compassion. We are destined to become as incense.

The language of mystics proves how futile it would be to separate spirituality from sensuousness. And why should we try to force a separation? Dull handbooks have tried this, but hardly with success. Sacred scriptures and mystical writings of every tradition bear witness to spiritual sensuousness and sensuous spirituality.

A privileged biblical image for sense perceived through the senses, yet surpassing the sensuous realm, is the Burning Bush (Ex. 3). A dried-out desert thornbush blazes into flame. Moses herding his sheep hears the fire crackling and turns. Amazed he asks himself, "why is this bush not burnt?" Many times before, he must have seen a bramble ignite in the desert noonday heat; in a flash, the bush would turn to ashes. What made this sight so strange was not the fire, but the preservation of tinder-dry wood in the midst of the fire. This "strange sight" (Ex. 3:3) signals a central theme of the whole Bible: God's presence in our midst, the co-existence, even more than that, the inter-penetration between what is accessible to our senses and what goes altogether beyond them. These two "suffer no confusion, but permit no separation" *(non confusionem passus, neque divisionem)* as a Christmas antiphon puts it, full of wonderment and awe. The image of the Burning Bush boldly proclaims: Divine Reality is accessible through the senses. This is quite a claim. It becomes even more striking as we read on.

Out of the fire a voice startles Moses: "Do not come closer!" A warning, no doubt, to keep a proper distance out of awe and sacred dread and reverence. This is one possible understanding. But another rabbinical tradition has reached a deeper insight: you do not *need* to come closer. Note that the voice continues: "Take off your shoes. The place on which you are standing is holy ground." You will become aware that you need not come closer, the moment you take off your shoes. You will re-alize that you are already standing on holy ground, the moment you remove the skin of dead animals which you have put between your live soles and the holy ground under your feet. The shoes stand for the very opposite of grateful sensuous aliveness. They symbolize deadness, insensibility, and taking-for-granted. Wherever we stand, we are standing on holy ground, but by insensibility we exile ourselves from the Holy Presence accessible through our senses. "What was the *real* exile?" the rabbis ask. "Was it Egypt? Was it Babylon? — No!" they answer, "It was: getting-used-to-it." Take off your shoes and return from exile: feel holy ground!

Walking barefoot — what better image for recovering the world of touch? "My foot converses with the stones on which it treads," says "The Blind Girl" in Rilke's poem (*Buch der Bilder* II: 2). Anyone's feet can learn to converse with the ground. As soon as we remove what gets in the way, be it shoes or thoughtless habit, we are in touch; conversation becomes possible. The Presence Beyond Words speaks to our sense of touch in countless different languages. To learn these languages is a delight. God in the wet meadow speaks to my feet in a language different from that of sun-warmed granite in the dry creek bed. The tile floor around the fountain speaks a cool language, like Latin. Hay that tickles my toes prattles like peasant children. My feet are fluent in the idiom of floorboards, doormats and all sorts of sand and pebbles on the beach.

Linen, leather, loofa — how differently each of them speaks to neck and shoulders. Straw hat and fur cap, beanie and helmet; pants loose and baggy or tights; how different their touch. Every area of our skin responds differently to different kinds of touch — brushing, scratching, rubbing, kneading, tickling, stroking. Yes, for our sense of touch, too, the fountains of blessing are filled to the brim.

Hands — as yet I haven't even mentioned hands: palms, thumbs, fingers, fingernails, fingertips. When I dust the chair in the hermitage, fingering the spaces between spindles at its back, this can be a series of caresses; I can do it as mindfully and lovingly as when I stroke Poppy, the cat. I remember Soen Roshi saying to us young monks, who thought of sweeping as something to get over and be done with: "That's no way to treat the dust. Your hands are to make the broom say to the dust, 'Sorry, you happen to be in a place where you don't belong; let me help you out.' " The language of hands can be rough or refined. Hands can be taught to be polite; this is part of sensuous asceticism.

Watch the hands of musicians tenderly touching their instruments. The gentle touch with which *The Guitarist Tunes Up* is a prototype of affectionate reverence. Frances Cornford (1886–1960) describes it in a poem with that title. "With what attentive courtesy he bent/over his instrument," she marvels, reminding us that a true master treats an instrument "not as a lordly conqueror," but with lovingly listening fingers. To listen with one's fingertips no less than with one's ears is the essence of obedience. Her guitarist behaves:

> ...as a man with a loved woman might
> Inquiring with delight
> What slight essential thing she had to say
>
> Before they started, he and she, to play.

The Japanese tea ceremony is a time-honored method for teaching hands to listen. Long ago, it was simply the way monks prepared a cup of whisked tea, served it to a guest, and washed the dishes — mindfully. Now, these three steps have become formalized in many different styles, and in Japan, every year, hundreds of thousands of students from all walks of life enroll in courses to study this sensuous ascetical practice.

It was a historic event when Sen Soshitsu, Japan's Grand Tea Master, visited New York. I knew that his ancestor, the great Sen Rikyu, had given the tea ceremony its classical form almost half a millennium ago. Of course, I was eager to meet Sen Rikyu's successor and descendant — the 16th in an unbroken line. But this soft-spoken gentleman with the hands of an artist proved to be far more than a celebrity distinguished by lineage and title. Here was a true master of sensuous asceticism. A small incident I was privileged to witness showed me this.

I still remember the reflections of city lights in the East River and in the rain-wet pavement of United Nations Plaza, twenty-two floors below the candle-lit apartment where a reception for Mr. and Mrs. Sen had been prepared with exquisite taste. Their hosts wanted to treat the honored guests from the East to the finest of Western culture. A famous keyboard artist had been engaged to play on a harpsichord rented for this occasion. There the instrument stood in all its elegant simplicity, its wood aglow in the light of candelabra. But it was locked and a whisper was going around that the key to the fallboard was nowhere to be found. Time for the performance came closer. The guests started whispering, getting flustered, embarrassed, tense. Finally everyone fell silent. The Tea Master caught on. Calmly he walked up to the harpsichord, stretched out his slender hand and passed his palm over the silky surface of the lid, back and forth, quite a few times. Then he looked up at us, smiled, and the spell was broken. All possible music seemed to have streamed from the silent harpsichord through these listening hands into his all embracing smile. We were in touch. All of us felt held by a firm but gentle embrace.

Touching is always mutual. We are able to see without being seen (children like to peek); we can hear without being heard, and smell without (we hope) emitting a smell; but no one can touch without being touched. This is so obvious that we take it for granted. Yet, it adds a new aspect to my contention that personal ascetical practice leads to social change. People who practice mindful looking will see what needs to be done in the world; those who learn to listen will hear the challenges which social evils shout at us; noses that come alive will smell it when "something is rotten in the State of Denmark." But to be in touch with the world around us goes one step further: it puts us in touch with the sore spots of our society, and this contact will prove to be a mutually healing touch. Being out of touch makes one sick. Touch heals. We need not fear contact, only the lack of it. It is not contact that leads to violence, but alienation. When we create a gap between highly charged poles, a lethal spark is bound to jump. Contact, even friction, allows the charge to flow rather than build up to dangerously high voltage. Touch keeps blessing in flow. The more alert we become to the blessing that flows into us through everything we touch, the more our own touch will bring blessing.

> *Being out of touch makes one sick. Touch is healing. We need not fear contact, only lack of it.*

Sensuous Asceticism

Only one sensation puts us in even closer touch than touching: tasting. Seeing allows for a great distance from what we see — an unimaginably vast distance, in fact. Standing under the night sky, we look at stars so far away that the light we now see started travelling when dinosaurs were still roaming on Earth. Our range of hearing is incomparably closer, our range of smelling closer still. Touching allows for no distance at all, yet it gives only surface contact. But tasting what dissolves on our tongue dissolves the barriers between subject and object. What we have tasted we know "inside out." No wonder, tasting became a metaphor for sapiential knowing. *Sapientia,* the Latin word for wisdom, means quite literally the ability to taste.

Nothing will reveal the world to us as intimately as savoring its bittersweet taste. To live to the full is to "taste life." To die consciously is to "taste death." In that same idiom the Psalmist encourages all who seek wisdom to "taste and see that the Lord is good" (Ps. 34:9). In this passage, tasting refers to our senses, the rabbis point out; seeing, to our intellect. These two must not be separated. Wisdom demands both tasting and seeing. Without sensuous experience the intellect can at best acquire book learning. But Lady Wisdom, as the Bible depicts her, with all her perfumes, ointments, spices, and tasty dishes leads us through "tasting life" with all our senses to "seeing life" in a light for which only the heart has eyes.

We met Holy Wisdom a few pages back in connection with ascetical training of the sense of smell. Tasting and smelling are as close to each other as mouth and nose. What loss it would be if we could not also smell the food we taste. Yet, what many consider the most important taste of all has no smell. "The nose knows not the savor of salt," a proverb of the Hausa of Nigeria reminds us. Salt is an ancient and widespread symbol for wisdom. Salt brings out the taste of food for the body, wisdom for the mind.

Salt preserves food from corruption; since stench and decay were associated with demonic influence, salt came to stand for divine blessing. So sacred was salt held to be that "every sacrifice must be salted with salt" (Lev. 2:13, Mk. 9:50). In the act of immolation incense and salt fuse into one symbol. Sacrifice expresses transformation. The ascetical path of wisdom and compassion cannot bypass sacrifice. From giving oneself *to* blessing this path leads to giving oneself *as* blessing. Those who follow the path of sensuous asceticism will become "the salt of the Earth" (Mt. 5:13), a blessing for the whole world; but first they must be "salted with fire" (Mk. 9:49), with transforming fire in which wisdom becomes fully itself by becoming compassion.

Every meal worth its salt is worth being eaten mindfully, worth being tasted with wisdom. My Buddhist friends chant before meals: "Innumerable labors brought us this food; we should know how it comes to us." Do we know it? Do we think of the innumerable creatures who labored and suffered and died to provide us with food? The practice of cultivating our sense of taste ought to include this dimension, too. Listing fruits, "apple, pear, gooseberry, banana ..." Rilke marveled, "All this speaks/ death and life into your mouth" *(Sonnets to Orpheus,* I: 13). Have you ever thought of your mouth as being spoken into like the mouthpiece of a telephone? "Where words used to be, discoveries gush forth" *(ibid.),* discoveries not only of life, but also of death, the death on

which we feed and the life that finds fulfillment in becoming food for others.

"We eat to support life," Buddhist monks remind
themselves in their chant before a meal. We eat to support our own life and the life of others who eat us up —
metaphorically and, eventually, literally. The food chain
is a closed circle. On the biological level we humans are
but one link in that chain. Wisdom will taste life and death
with full awareness and will relish their tart intermingling.
But wisdom has a wider perspective. Wisdom can see a
food chain, as it were, that transcends biological life —
not a closed circle, but an ever-rising helix. Fr. George
Kosicki tells a delightfully whimsical story about this.

Once upon a time, there was a dandelion growing in
a meadow. The dandelion whispered to the amino acids
and all the other nutrients in the soil, "How would you
like to become dandelion? You need only to allow your-
selves to be dissolved in a drop of water and I will suck
you up through my roots. You won't feel a thing. But afterwards, you will be able to grow and to flower and to
fly away in the wind as a thousand miniature parachutes
carrying seed." "Okay," said the amino acids and other
nutrients in the soil. They let themselves be dissolved in
rainwater and sucked up through the roots and they became dandelion.

The next morning, a rabbit came hopping across the
meadow. "Good morning!" said the rabbit to the dandelion, "How would you like to become rabbit? You will have
to allow yourself to be nibbled and chewed and swal-
lowed. It hurts a little, but afterwards you will be able to
jump and bounce and romp in the moonlight, wiggle your
ears, and have lots of baby rabbits." The dandelion was
not overly enthusiastic, but the idea of hopping around

sounded like a lot more fun than being stuck in one place. "Okay," said the dandelion with a sigh. It allowed itself to be munched and became rabbit.

Towards evening, a hunter came by. "Good morning!" said the hunter to the rabbit (for it was an unusually polite hunter), "How would you like to become human? You must allow yourself to be shot dead, skinned, cooked in a stew, and eaten. This is not pleasant, I admit, but imagine, afterwards you will be able to play yo-yo, sing in the shower, and fly in a jet-plane." The rabbit was scared, but flying in a jet-plane seemed so exciting; the idea was irresistible. Sniffling a little and wiping away a tear, the rabbit mumbled, "O.K.," went through with that ordeal and became human.

But then, God came along. "Hi!" God said. "How would you like to become...?"

Am I willing to pay the price T. S. Eliot spoke of — "A condition of complete simplicity / (Costing not less than everything)"? *(Four Quartets,* IV:V:253). Do I dare to move towards this goal along the trajectory of courage set up by amino acids, dandelion, and rabbit in the story? The process becomes more and more demanding, yet also more and more fulfilling. Through sensuous asceticism We learn to meet the demands with courage; we learn to see the fulfillment not as achievement, but as pure gift. Our ultimate courage is merely the brave trust to accept the ultimate gift: transformation into that which unawares we *are.*

Mirror of the Heart

Haiku poetry is in itself an inexhaustible topic. To discover it, to enter more deeply into it, to revel in its delights would be worthwhile in itself. But what I would like to consider here is the function of the Haiku as a mirror. Like a crystal, the facets of which mirror and bring together so many different reflections of the world around it, the Haiku shows us some important aspects of our human world gathered together and reflected as if in one brief sparkling flash. The clarity and precision of this remarkable poetic form are only heightened by the fact that it is so utterly unsentimental. So is a mirror.

The Haiku as mirror for human self-understanding will have its function whenever this self-understanding tends to get blurred. Yet, in our time it may be particularly helpful. For one thing it is an Eastern form of poetry reaching the West precisely at the moment when one great task before us is bridge-building between East and West. And it is a poem of awareness. Among all poetic forms there is not one in which awareness is more central than in the Haiku, and this at a time when we are discovering new horizons of awareness both in outer and in inner space. In this awareness, the Haiku never loses sight of the paradox of time and space, and this, too, makes it particularly helpful for our own new self-awareness. For as Albert Einstein and T. S. Eliot have pointed out to us from vastly different vantage points, the paradox of time and space lies at the core of our new confrontation with the paradox of human existence.

The Haiku thus becomes a many-faceted mirror in which we may look for deeper understanding of the human paradox. And this suggests the way in which we might go about building this essay. We must begin with experience, your own experience, if possible, and so at the outset we shall try to get to some experience of your own — one of those experiences in which the human paradox comes to a peak. We shall explore this Peak Experience in the hope of discovering some key aspects for a deeper understanding of it. T. S. Eliot will help us in this, for he faces directly, and in a way that is more familiar to Westerners, the same paradox that the Haiku reflects indirectly. This will be our next step: to examine just how the various aspects of the human paradox are reflected in the crystal of the Haiku.

We shall let the Haiku speak for itself as far as possible, but as we listen to it and allow ourselves to swing with it, we shall become aware of its preponderance towards one pole of our experience — its "still point." And this shall provide us, unexpectedly for some maybe, with a key for understanding monastic life. Surprising as the connection between Haiku and monastic life may appear, it stands on solid ground. The human paradox discovered in the peak experience, and crystallized in the Haiku, is lived out in monastic life as one of its paradigmatic forms. This is what provides the connection. The new self-understanding for which our time is groping and towards which the Haiku can help us is simply incomplete without the contemplative dimension, or to put it more concretely, without the discovery of the monk in each one of us.

But we have a long way to go, and we must start, as we have said, with experience, and this as close to home as possible with a peak experience of our own. The term *Peak Experience* is a good one, and a useful one. For we do experience our lives as relatively long stretches of ascent and decline culminating here and there in brief moments for which a peak is the perfect image. But like every term, the term lends itself to empty manipulation, and this would be futile. To use the term well, we must fill it with content from the well of our own experience. We are setting out on an exploration of inner space — your own, and we won't settle for less.

May I suggest, then, that you take your eyes off the page now and then. Closing your eyes, you might recall and relive one of those major or minor peaks of your past experience. Try to focus on a moment of which you can truly say that it made your life worthwhile, not for others (this would put us on the wrong track here) but for yourself. Seen from one of these peaks, the long stretches of ascent were suddenly meaningful, the slopes of decline appeared bearable: life was seen as worth living.

Maybe it was even outwardly a moment on a mountain top, at sunset, it could be, or in the brisk brilliance of an autumn day. Maybe it was a passage in a book, a poem, or a melody that lifted you up onto an inner peak, unnoticed by anyone else. Or sitting on a fence-rail dangling your legs, not in boredom, not at all, but in utter absorption. Absorption into what? Into nothing; for nothing happened. And those moments mark our highest peaks, those moments when nothing does indeed happen to us. If this last point puzzles you, don't give up too quickly. All that matters for the moment is that you set your mind on a peak experience of your own, a specific one against which you can check my suggestions. For I will suggest, in outline, some aspects of the dynamic event which took place at that moment. You must check for yourself how this outline applies.

What makes it so different to reflect on the moment of our Peak Experience is that it is in itself an altogether unreflective moment. This is, in fact, its main characteristic. What makes the Peak Experience so liberating is that precisely for once I no longer feel that I feel and know that I know, but simply feel and know, and just that. Only afterwards can I reflect on it and so talk about it. And what I am then inclined to say is something like, "I was simply swept off my feet," or "I was out of myself, carried away."

Not to feel that you feel, not to know that you know, but just to feel, just to know— how liberating!

Even though it might have been for a split second only, "I had lost myself." This was all. But not quite all. For looking back I will also admit that at the moment of my Peak Experience I was more truly and more fully myself than at any other time. And so I find myself confronted with the strange paradox that I am most truly myself when I forget myself. When I lose myself, I find my Self.

This paradoxical tension between self and Self, between losing and finding, is paralleled (and this is the second aspect) by another facet of the paradox, and you can check this, too, against your own experience. It matters little whether the experience you have in mind took place on a lonely mountain, say, or in the midst of a crowded concert hall. At the peak moment you were alone in a deep sense. Not that you were reflecting on it then and there, but reflecting on it later you find that the word *alone* applies, even though there may have been a crowd around you. You were in some sense "the only one." You were, and this is even more important, not only singled out but of a single mind; and so you were "alone" also in the sense of being altogether with yourself, all of one piece, "all one."

But this second facet of our paradox also implies a tension. Precisely as you were all one with yourself, you experienced keenly being one with all. Your profound solitude was matched by limitless togetherness. In fact, the two were simply two aspects of the same experience. And again it matters little whether externally you were alone or in a crowd. Even alone on an island, miles away from other human beings, you may have been overwhelmed by the awareness of a deep union with everyone. Nor was this togetherness limited to people. At this melting point your innermost being had fused into the fragrance of the wild thyme in the evening meadow, into the sudden flash of winter lightning, into the voice of the waterfall or of the flute. You were alone, all one, one with all.

There was nothing to be said at that point. It is only afterwards that we are putting all of this into words, limping words at that, words that will never catch up with our experience. But in some sense you yourself were a word at that crucial moment, a word more simple and immediate than words are once they have surfaced into language. This word will necessarily lose in translation but if we must attempt translating it, what comes closest might be simply "Ah!" or "Wow!" or "Yes!" or "This is it!" — an exclamation of awe-filled affirmation. You had somehow gone beyond reasoning and suddenly everything made sense. This is a third facet of our paradoxical Peak Experience. No questions asked, no answers given, and yet everything appears right, just as it is. Chinese wisdom caught this insight in a saying which is as simple as it is deep: "The beautiful snow never falls onto an inappropriate place." Indeed, this is merely a more elaborate way of saying "This is it!"

When I exclaim "This is it!" the meaning of "it" is simply without limit. It means life and death, it means the whole universe and it stretches out to anything that may lie beyond it. It stands for ultimate meaning. And yet what I have discovered is not an abstraction but this concrete thing before me, a thing that is meaningful, full of meaning, and so I am never quite sure of where to put the accent of my "This is it!"

> *I lose myself:*
> *I find myself.*
> *I am alone:*
> *I am one with all.*
> *I stop questioning:*
> *I am the answer.*

The emphasis hovers between "This is IT" on the one hand, and "THIS is it!" on the other. A moment ago we stressed the "IT," the overpowering meaning revealed in our experience. Now we stress the "THIS," the thing or situation at hand in all its concreteness. And by this switch we realize that the meaning is not, as it were, behind this thing, or above, or beyond, or inside it.

The thing or situation is simply a word or sign that embodies its significance. It is simply the shape of its meaning. This fragrance of wild thyme, this tone of a flute is simply one shape of Ultimate Reality. I cannot decide where to place the accent. All I am sure of is that "This IS it!"

A Haiku does not talk about an experience; a Haiku triggers an experience — your own.

I hope that you were able to check these aspects of a Peak Experience step by step against your own. Yet all this is still mere talk about experience, and I apologize. Poets don't talk about an experience. They let it come to word. That's quite a different way of approach, and this is where we come to Haiku.

Much must be presupposed here, and much may be presupposed, for excellent introductions to Haiku poetry are easily available in English. But through our reflections on the Peak Experience, we have gained access to Haiku from within, as it were. If you have become aware that you are most truly yourself when you forget yourself; that in truly being alone you are one with all; that everything makes sense as soon as you go beyond reasoning; you have discovered in your own experience the paradox in which Haiku has its roots.

Not that the Masters of Haiku would try to "capture" a Peak Experience (a Western poet might try to do this);

what they are trying to do is not to capture the experience, but to set it free — to stimulate you just barely enough to bring back an experience of your own. A master of Haiku will make the reader his co-poet. "We had the experience but missed the meaning." Now, seen in the mirror of Haiku, "the hint half guessed, the gift half understood..." that had been granted to us at last yields its meaning. The poet offers you a mirror, but a mirror without light is empty and dark. The light that flashes in the crystal mirror of Haiku must be the light of your own experience.

But here we are already in the midst of paradox. Did we not say that you had "lost yourself" at the climax of your Peak Experience? Where were you when you were "swept off your feet"? Nowhere and everywhere. How then can the Haiku bring you back to the place that was no place? To that time that was out of time? It does so, paradoxically, by bringing you to a most specific place at a most specific time. (Here lies, incidentally, the importance of the so-called "season word" of classical Haiku.) Vagueness is incompatible with Haiku, because it is altogether incompatible with "the sudden illumination" of the Peak Experience. And the "season word," far from being a literary convention, aims at that bursting of space and time which, paradoxically, coincides with the ultimate clarity and precision of the here and now. It is a strange coincidence that the English word *nowhere* is a fusion of *now* and *here.* "You cannot face it steadily," but if, for one brief now you are truly here (wherever this may be), you are nowhere because you are everywhere.

> Here, the intersection of the timeless moment,
> Is England and nowhere. Never and always.[1]

How, then, can the Haiku help you recover "the point of intersection of the timeless with time"? The point where "all is always now"? How? Simply by leaving room. Not by what is said, but by what is left unsaid. This Haiku, for instance, takes shape just at the point where reflection returns, and I, reentering the orbit of my little self, become aware that I had gone beyond.

> *The butterfly has disappeared*
> *And now it comes back to me,*
> *My wandering mind.*

Who is to capture the moment in which you have lost yourself? The moment of which reflexive awareness can take hold is only the moment after, the moment of return — from where?

> I can only say, *there* we have been:
>   but I cannot say where.
> And I cannot say, how long, for that is to
>   place it in time.[2]

And what is it that "comes back to you"? Is it the butterfly or your wandering mind? We are left in suspense. Who can tell in the end? Who needs to tell?

All this may have taken place in a flash. But in another Haiku, the poet suggests a losing of self in wonderment, sustained, maybe, for hours throughout a moonlit night.

> *The moon in the pines*
> *Now I hang it up, now I take it off*
> *And still I keep gazing.*

Again that delicate suspense which here pivots on the little word "still." Is it in stillness that I am gazing? Am I still gazing on and on after "hanging" the moon on this branch or that? Or, and this to me is the most intriguing possibility, am I still gazing after having taken down the moon, gazing at nothing, and still gazing?

But just to make sure that moon and butterflies and the moods they evoke are not at all essential to the kind of experience typical for a Haiku let me give you a very different one, still in the context of losing oneself. Here the setting is refreshingly active: rows of farm workers hoeing fields on a distant hill, rhythmically swinging their mattocks.

> *Up they swing*
> *And the mattocks glitter:*
> *Fields in spring.*

What a virile image of spring! That fraction of a moment in which the sun flashes on a shining blade, here and now sparks an explosion of power and joy, bursting your little self, catapulting you to that "still point" where "All is always now."[3]

It takes only a slight shift of emphasis, and the point of aloneness in dynamic stillness becomes the point of consummate union. The butterfly, in whose flight I had lost myself, unified my vision, for by taking me out of myself, it made me one with all, and healed me of duality. And now that almost imperceptible shift of emphasis:

> *Down the barley rows*
> *Stitching, stitching them together*
> *The butterfly goes.*

In a moment of celebration, this butterfly restores aloneness to all-oneness. As I am watching it, stitching the barley rows together, I lose myself and realize the profound paradox hinted at by the English word "alone" — "all-one." To be truly alone is not at all to be lonely, for the heart of my heart, that secret place where I am most intimately myself, is, paradoxically, the point where I am also the most intimately one with all other human beings, with all living beings, with the Source of being. To be truly alone is to be healed of duality, one with my true Self, and thus one with all.

To be alone in this sense is to have reached what T. S. Eliot calls "the still point of the turning world," the still point of the Great Dance, the peak "where past and future are gathered."

> Neither movement from nor towards,
> Neither ascent nor decline.
> Except for the point, the still point,
> There would be no dance, and there is
> only the dance.[4]

Let us look at another Haiku:

Five blue butterflies
Summer roadside festival
Dusty boots stand still.

Here, again, the meaning pivots on the ambiguity of the words "stand still." Is this an imperative? Is the poet saying, "For heaven's sake, here it is, the Great Dance? It doesn't take more than a handful of those commonest of all butterflies, the tiny blue ones rarely seen on flowers, but content to put on their summer festival in the ruts of dirt roads running through summer fields. Here it is, the still point of the Great Dance, and it is all yours if only you will stand still!" Or is this again a fully accomplished instance of self lost and Self found, the all-oneness of the solitary traveler whose dusty boots stand still, at long last, "at the still point of the turning world," "and there is only the Dance"?

The lake is lost
In the rain which is lost
In the lake.

They blossom, and then
We gaze, and then the blossoms
Scatter, and then....

The pain of blissful aloneness and the bliss of the pain that makes all one keenly coincide in the peak of the Peak Experience, in the still point, in the Haiku.

93

Mirror of the Heart

The moments of happiness...

We had the experience but missed the meaning,
And approach to the meaning restores the experience
In a different form, beyond any meaning
We can assign to happiness.[5]

Pain and bliss are reconciled, all opposites are reconciled, and we are reconciled to the paradox that the opposites coincide. Duality is not eliminated but healed, overcome in solitude-togetherness. Without argument, without reasoning everything suddenly makes sense. We can say "Yes" to paradox.

But this is not a "Yes" of resignation. It is a "Yes" of triumph, an unlimited "Yes" to reality, to Ultimate Reality. It is a "Yes" pregnant with newness of discovery. Our ears are popping; our eyes pop open and see all the familiar things as if we had never seen them before:

Green fields of grain:
A sky-lark rises over there.
Comes down again.

As the spring rains fall,
Soaking in them, on the roof,
Is a child's rag ball.

This freshness of vision may rise to a crescendo of surprise at the most ordinary things. So in the wildest of all the Haiku I know: here the overabundance of cherry blossoms so fills the poet with sober inebriation that he looks even at horses and birds as if it were for the first time in his life.

> *Cherry blossoms, more*
> *And more now! birds have two legs!*
> *Oh, horses have four!*

The directness and immediacy that is so overpowering here is possibly the most striking characteristic both of the Peak Experience and of the Haiku. No abstractions here!

> *They rolled out too far*
> *From their leaf shelter, melons —*
> *And how hot they are!*

> *Truckloads of pumpkins*
> *Swishing by. And in the dust*
> *One busted pumpkin.*

One melon, one pumpkin — we see it, we feel it, our whole being says "Yes, this is it," and we have said "Yes" to the whole universe. What is more marvelous, that the meaning of the whole universe gives itself to us in one pumpkin, or that one pumpkin can convey to us the meaning of the whole universe? We need not decide. The marvel lies in the coincidence of the two: that ultimate meaning should be so concrete and that this concrete thing should be so ultimately meaningful.

Between the lightning flash seen and the impact of its meaning perceived, there must not be the slightest crack or crevice into which reflexive thinking could insert itself. This would destroy the immediacy of the experience. This is the burden of Basho's famous statement: "When the lightning flashes, how admirable he who does *not* think: life is fleeting." To think it would mean to "overstand" rather than "understand," grasp one aspect of the experience rather than being "grabbed" by its total impact. Understanding hinges on the directness of our insight, "This IS it!"

It is with the meaning revealed in the Peak Experience that the Haiku is ultimately concerned. Not, of course — and this should be clear from all that we have said — as if the meaning could be separated from the word that gives it expression. The meaning is not another word behind the word. Meaning is silence. It comes to itself as it finds form. It finds form as it comes to word, but meaning, as such, is silent. And "Words, after speech, reach into silence."[6]

The Haiku is, paradoxically, a poem about silence. Its very core is silence. There is probably no shorter poetic form in world literature than the classical Haiku with its seventeen syllables and, yet, the masters put these seventeen syllables down with a gesture of apology, which makes it clear that the words merely serve the silence. All that matters is the silence. The Haiku is a scaffold of words; what is being constructed is a poem of silence; and when it is ready, the poet gives a little kick, as it were, to the scaffold. It tumbles, and silence alone stands.

> *Evening rain*
> *The banana leaf*
> *Speaks of it first.*

We can almost hear the first big raindrops falling one by one. But this is already the moment after the decisive one; the moment after the one that held its breath in limitless anticipation. This is not a poem about rain, but about the silence before the rain. A strange poem, the Haiku! It zeroes in on the here and now which is nowhere. It celebrates the all-oneness of aloneness in all the bliss of its poignant pain. It stakes out territory for discovery precisely where life is most daily. And while setting up landmarks of adventure, it wipes out its own footprints. It denies itself. For it shoots words like arrows at the target of silence. Every word that hits the mark returns to the silence out of which it has come.

Does this sound paradoxical? It certainly is, yet, no more paradoxical than you are to yourself. For the Haiku merely mirrors the paradox of the "still point" — the paradox of the human heart. In a masterly Haiku what it means to be human has been crystallized. Crystallized, not petrified. Not like rock, but lightly as in a snowflake that will melt and become a drop of water as soon as it touches you. Crystallized in the Haiku, the paradox is not dispelled. It is brought home; it is made bearable; you can stand under it and rejoice in it as children rejoice in snowflakes. And thus, standing for once under the paradox rather than over against it, you can understand; you can understand yourself.

Self-understanding attained at the "still point"; this is the core of the Peak Experience; the burden of T. S. Eliot's *Four Quartets;* the hidden source of Haiku poetry; the goal of the monk. Of course, the goal is the same for all of us, and monastic life is but one possible way of attaining this goal. But in its form, monastic life is paradigmatic, allowing us to trace the human paradox in a few broad strokes.

This is the reason why in today's identity crisis many turn with renewed interest toward monastic tradition. Those whose interest turns in this direction will hardly be able to find a more direct approach to understanding monastic life than the one attempted here. For as long as we try to find access to it from the outside, we won't get beyond highly complex socio-religious phenomena in history; we won't get beyond labels. But approached from within, along the lines suggested here, the monastic quest will be seen to be much more than a periodically recurring fringe phenomenon of organized religion. It will reveal itself as one possible way of realizing a basic human dimension, the exploration of inner space; something pursued by few but in behalf of all; something that concerns each one of us. And, in a measure, it can be understood by every human being.

> ...the moment in and out of time,
> The distraction fit, lost in a shaft of sunlight,
> The wild thyme unseen, or the winter lightning
> Or the waterfall, or music heard so deeply
> That it is not heard at all, but you are the music
> While the music lasts.[7]

If you have experienced, no matter how marginally, the painful bliss of it all, why not concede the possibility that others might attempt to center their whole life on this one goal:

> ...to apprehend
> The point of intersection of the timeless
> With time....[8]

(They may be eccentrics, granted. In fact, one might have to be eccentric in order to feel so strong a need for zeroing in on this center "at the still point." So what? A need is always the reverse side of a talent.)

And if you have experienced the rich aloneness that, though it be for one moment, only dissolves all limits to your oneness with the universe, why not concede the possibility that someone may choose to become a "loner" for the sake of becoming a "brother" to brother wolf and to brother sun, to sister water and to sister death? (After all, *monachos* means literally "loner," and yet, it is the monk whom everyone calls "brother.")

And, again, if you have seen in a flash that everything makes sense as soon as you go beyond reasoning, you will be ready to understand why some men and women should devote their whole life to the pursuit of this paradox. What they are seeking is:

> ...Not the intense moment
> Isolated, with no before and after,
> But a lifetime burning in every moment.

> ...But to apprehend
> The point of intersection of the timeless
> With time, is an occupation for the saint—
> No occupation either, but something given
> And taken, in a lifetime's death in love,
> Ardor and selflessness and self-surrender.

Mirror of the Heart

For most of us, this is the aim
Never here to be realized;
Who are only undefeated
Because we have gone on trying;[9]

For us, there is only the trying.
The rest is not our business.[10]

The road of monks is but one of the possible roads of approach to the "still point," but it is an approach by which, for a long time, many have made their way. And while some basic experience of the human paradox is necessary to understand the forms of monastic tradition from within, the forms of life that the monks have cultivated may in turn aid us in our understanding of the human paradox.

As we have seen, the human paradox flares up in a sudden flash of self-understanding "at the still point" of the Peak Experience. It happens. No effort we could make would earn for us this experience. It is *gratis: gratia gratis data* — a gift, always. What, then, can we do towards it? We can prepare ourselves. And how? The monk's answer is: by training. An ascetic is one who trains. (The Greek word *askein* means "to exercise," and since this exercise is purposeful, we translate, "to train.") This is what asceticism is: goal-directed, systematic training. And the goal is to discover, again and again, "the still point."

No wonder, then, that some decisive strokes, characteristic for the ascetic tradition, should correspond to lines we have been able to trace in the Peak Experience. Thus, we shall encounter again the paradox of a here-and-now intensified beyond space and time. The particular form this paradox assumes in ascetic life is "detachment" (never to be confused with indifference). We shall also find again the paradox of solitude and togetherness, and its particular form will be ascetic "celibacy." And we shall meet again the "this-is-it" experience in all its paradoxical tension. The peculiar accentuation of this tension characteristic of ascetic life gives rise to a whole life-style marked by silence, mindfulness, prayer, celebration. What lies at the root of this life-style is "obedience" — in a much more comprehensive sense, obviously, than obedience has in everyday language — obedience as a constantly renewed listening to the meaning of each moment. All three — detachment, celibacy, and obedience — are directly related to the quest for the "still point."

We have said "detachment," but any connotation of indifference must be completely ruled out. Any resemblance between indifference and detachment is mere deception. For detachment is not a withdrawal from love, but an expansion of love beyond desire. Desire is entangled in time, nostalgic for the past, preoccupied with the future. Love expanding beyond desire is "liberation from the future as well as the past." What remains is the *now* "where past and future are gathered," the "still point."

In our own daily life we may experience the liberating expansion of love. In fact, we may come to find our own actions less and less important, yet — another paradox — even more significant, as the context in which they are seen expands. This is what happens along the way of monastic detachment: the here and now gains in significance precisely in proportion to the loss of its importance. "At the still point" here and now cease to matter and attain ultimate significance. A "secluded chapel," a "winter's afternoon" become "England and nowhere. Never and always."[11] This implies that training in detachment must aim at cultivating its own awareness of space and time. Nothing short of this will do.

The various forms by which monks of different traditions cultivate the ascetic approach to space, for instance, may appear poles apart from one another. But once we have the clue, it is easy to see that the goal is the same. Forms as different from one another as the homelessness of the pilgrim monk and stability in the cloister are merely two ways to the same goal. A wayfaring monk on the roads of India, or a stylite who spends his life on a pillar; the Irish monks of the Middle Ages seafaring across the northern Atlantic, or the walled-in recluses in ancient Russia; and all those monks whose form of life falls somewhere between these extremes — they all simply aim at this: being present where they are, truly, totally present.

> ...In order to arrive there,
> To arrive where you are,
>   to get from where you are not,
>   You must go by a way wherein there is no ecstasy.[12]

"Ecstasy" literally denotes a "being beside oneself," put out of place, even deranged — the very opposite of that total centeredness, that full presence where you are, with both feet on the ground, in a given "instant." That the "ecstasy" should happen at the very "instant" is merely the linguistic reflection of the paradox with which we are here concerned. There is the ecstatic instant, but there is no instant ecstasy. Monastic training is unhurried and down to earth: sweeping, cooking, washing; serving at table or at the altar; reading books or filing library cards; digging, typing, haying, plumbing — but all of this with that affectionate detachment which makes the place where you are the navel of the universe.

To this monastic awareness of place belongs a distinctively monastic awareness of time.

> The time of the seasons and the constellations
> The time of milking and the time of harvest....[13]

The time of "the sea bell's perpetual angelus" on the coast where

> The tolling bell
> Measures time not our time, rung by the unhurried
> Ground swell, a time
> Older than the time of chronometers, older
> Than time counted....[14]

And the "unhurried ground swell" becomes an image of that "love expanding beyond desire," detached but not indifferent, on the contrary, alert and responsible — for the time measured by the tolling bell is "not our time." We are called. We must respond.

> And the ground swell,
>   that is and was from the beginning,
> Clangs
> The bell.[15]

The angelus bell and the gong, the clapper, the drum, the sounding board are so many ways of keeping time "not our time." This is the decisive point: that it is "not our time." The monks rise and go to sleep, work and celebrate, when "it is time." They are only "keeping" the time, not "setting" it. At the first sound of the bell, the monk is to let loose whatever he is engaged in, and turn to that for which it is time. What matters is the letting loose. It is liberation. Through it the time which was "not our time," all time, becomes ours because we give ourselves to it. Swinging with the living seasons you are "in tune with the world," and it is all yours.

This detachment from time and place through which everything becomes ours because we are fully present in the here and now, this is the seed fruit of monastic detachment, its ultimate accomplishment containing in seed everything.

> A condition of complete simplicity
> (Costing not less than everything.)[16]

All other renunciation is included in the monk's affectionate detachment from the here and now. It points to that ultimate self-detachment in which our true Self is found.

> In order to possess what you do not possess
> You must go by the way of dispossession.
> In order to arrive at what you are not
> You must go through the way in which you are not.[17]

Detachment, understood in this truly catholic, i.e., all-embracing sense, leads us directly to monastic celibacy, because

> Love is most nearly itself
> When here and now cease to matter.[18]

Celibacy certainly belongs in the context of "expanding of love beyond desire, and so, liberation."[19] Seen in this light, the accent switches from the aspect of dispossession, deprivation, renunciation to the aspect of expansion, liberation, fulfillment. In the context of the Peak Experience it makes sense to say that the monk is a celibate, a loner, because his oneness with all is expanding beyond desire. And it is equally true to say that he can embrace this oneness with all only because (and in so far as) he is truly alone. Celibacy is the daring attempt to sustain the "condition of extreme simplicity" in which solitude and togetherness merge so that aloneness becomes all-oneness.

This experience of concord with oneself and with all, a concord realized at the heart of the universe, at the still point — this experience is always granted *gratis*. But it is one thing to be surprised by it in a flash in the "moment of happiness ... the sudden illumination" and quite a different thing to sustain a life centered on this still point, to remain "still and still moving." For this we need the support of others embarked on the same venture. (Even the hermit needs this support, though less tangibly.) Monastic solitude must be supported by togetherness.

It is surprising how much togetherness one needs in order to save aloneness from deteriorating into loneliness. Here lies the root of monastic community. Solitude and togetherness make each other possible. Take away solitude, and togetherness becomes subhuman gregariousness; take away togetherness and solitude becomes desolation. Community can only exist in the tension between solitude and togetherness. The delicate balance between solitude and togetherness will determine what kind of community it shall be. In the togetherness community of which married life is the prototype, togetherness is the measure of solitude: each of the partners must have as much solitude as they need for rich and full togetherness. In the solitude community of monastic life, solitude is the measure of togetherness: here each partner must have just enough togetherness to enrich and support solitude. Monks in community help one another in love to cultivate and sustain genuine aloneness.

No one can do without this support. Even solitary explorers must still rely on the team that stands behind them. The stakes of this exploration are high. Celibate life means

> ...a trip that will be unpayable
> For a haul that will not bear examination.[20]

Supported "at the still point," we must explore the togetherness dimension of solitude, the all-oneness of aloneness.

> We must be still and still moving
> Into another intensity
> For a further union, a deeper communion
> Through the dark cold and the empty desolation....[21]

> We shall not cease from exploration
> And the end of all our exploring
> Will be to arrive where we started
> And know the place for the first time.[22]

We shall "know," but to know in this way shall be "the haul that will not bear examination." It will be a kind of knowledge that goes beyond count, beyond measure; not a knowing of knowledge, but a knowing experience.

> ...There is, it seems to us,
> At best, only a limited value
> In the knowledge derived from experience.[23]

What monks are after is not "knowledge derived," but immediate knowledge; not the knowledge we can grasp, of which we can take hold, but the meaning that speaks to us in the experience, hits us, "grabs" us, takes hold of us. And just as we saw that "time, not our time" gives itself to us as soon as we let loose in detachment and give ourselves over to its liberating power, so the meaning for which we are searching in life gives itself to us as soon as we renounce the effort to grasp it and begin to listen to it. Knowledge tries to grasp; wisdom listens. Listening wisdom: that is obedience.

Obviously, obedience here is taken in its most comprehensive sense. We must not restrict obedience to the notion of "doing someone else's will." This may be a somewhat conspicuous aspect of monastic training, yet submission is not an end in itself. It is a means, and only one of various means. The end is obedience in its full sense as a loving listening to the meaning that comes to us through everything and every person and every situation. If obedience meant no more than doing someone else's will, it might merely replace my own whims by the whims of someone else, but monastic training is designed to liberate from whim altogether. The master helps the monk to become detached from self-will, but this is only the beginning. The real task is learning to listen. The very word *obedience* comes from *ob-audire,* which means to listen intently. Its opposite is to be utterly deaf, and the word for this is literally *ab-surdus*. Everything is absurd until we learn to listen to its meaning; until we become "all ears" in obedience.

In order to listen, you have to be silent. Silence, then, is another means towards the intent listening of obedience. We mean an inner silence, above all, but this implies an outward silence which expresses and supports the inner. Yet, monastic silence does not consist in the elimination of words, the elimination of noise. This process of elimination leads, at best, to the hush of a public library or of a morgue. Monastic silence is not dead silence; it is alive with the presence of mystery like the silence of a deep forest. It is like the silence of a forester totally mindful of the game he is stalking. And all this recollected silence is intent on one goal: "to apprehend the point of intersection of the timeless with time"[24]—the still point.

Monastic silence is not dead silence. It is silence alive with mystery, with presence.

Monastic mindfulness or recollection, like monastic silence, is directly related to obedience. It is not the grim *Memento Mori* as which it is sometimes seen. And yet, it is in a sense concerned with death, since death is precisely the ultimate point of intersection of the timeless with time. But the recollection of the monk is not a morbid preoccupation with one's last hour. It is mindfulness of the present hour, the here and now, the "inter-section time," and it is in this sense that "the time of death is every moment."[25] At any moment in which you are truly present, your recollected consciousness may shatter the time barrier and burst into *now*. The moment of total pres-ence, through recollec-tion, is "the moment in and out of time."[26] Thus "history is a pattern of timeless moments."[27] Through recollected mindfulness, practiced

> ***At any moment
> the fully present mind
> can shatter time
> and burst into
> Now.***

throughout a lifetime, whatever the present moment con-tains becomes "a symbol, a symbol perfected in death."[28] In monastic life everything becomes "a symbol" because we are learning to listen to its meaning.

Prayer is unlimited mindfulness. And this coincides with the most traditional notion of prayer while it broad-ens the concept immensely. For you have always known that you can "say your prayers" without really having prayed. And when we ask: "what is it, then, that makes prayers, prayer?" The answer is "recollection." (Mind-fulness means the same and is a term less worn by use and abuse.) If you say your prayers mindfully, you really pray. Well then, what really matters is obviously mind-fulness, recollection, openness. The gesture of the open hands, raised in prayer, is in typical contrast to the clenched grip that tries to hold on to things. Prayerful recollection is loving openness to receive the meaning conveyed by a given moment. Set times for prayer are certainly necessary to cultivate prayerfulness, but should we restrict prayer to set times? If we know what it means to say prayers mindfully, we ought to be able to do everything with the same mindfulness. And thus everything becomes prayer; everything becomes celebration. Everything becomes celebration as we learn to take things one by one, moment by moment; to single everything out for grateful consideration.

Seen in this light, prayer, too, is but another way of listening in obedience. Humility, silence, recollection, prayer, what holds all these ascetic practices together is obedience. Detachment makes the monk free for the "trip that will be unpayable." Celibacy is the way in which he sets sail. Obedience is the lifelong voyage of exploration.

Monastic life, in solitude community, is only one way, not the only one. We have said this before. A married man or woman might someday outline by similarly paradigmatic form how the self-finding in a self-losing, the paradox of oneness and aloneness, and the listening for the silent meaning of life express themselves in togetherness community. The points of resemblance with monastic life might turn out to be stunning. When you look at a circle of dancers from outside the circle, those nearest to you will appear to move in one direction, those farthest from you in the opposite one. Yet, contrary to appearance, all of them are moving in the same direction around the circle.

> And the way up is the way down, the way
> forward is the way back.[29]

Note: Those who would like to look up the passages I quoted from T. S. Eliot's *Four Quartets* in their original context will find them listed here. The first Roman numeral stands for the poem (I *Burnt Norton;* II *East Coker;* III *The Dry Salvages;* IV *Little Gidding*); the second for the section within the poem. Arabic numerals indicate the lines.

1	IV:I:52f	17	II:III:140f
2	I:II:68f	18	II:V:200f
3	I:V:149	19	IV:III:157f
4	I:II:65-67	20	III:II:78f
5	III:II:89 & 92-95	21	II:V:204
6	I:V:139f	22	IV:V:239-242
7	III:V:207-212	23	II:II:81-83
8	III:V:200-202	24	III:V:200-202
9	III:V:226-229	25	III:III:159
10	III:V:189	26	III:V:207
11	IV:I:53	27	IV:V:234f
12	II:III:137f	28	IV:III:194f
13	II:I:42f	29	III:III:129
14	III:I:34-39		
15	III:I:46-48		
16	IV:V:253f		

A Deep Bow

People often ask me how Buddhists answer the question "Does God exist?"

The other day I was walking along the river. The wind was blowing. Suddenly I thought, oh! the air really exists. We know that the air is there, but unless the wind blows against our face, we are not aware of it. Here in the wind I was suddenly aware, yes it's really there.

And the sun too. I was suddenly aware of the sun, shining through the bare trees. Its warmth, its brightness; and all this completely free, completely gratuitous, simply there for us to enjoy.

And without my knowing it, completely spontaneously, my two hands came together, and I realized that I was making gassho. And it occurred to me that this is all that matters: that we can bow, take a deep bow. Just that. Just that.

—*The Reverend Eido Tai Shimano*

If we were able to experience this fundamental gratitude at all times, there would be no need to talk about it, and many of the contradictions that divide our world would at once be resolved. But in our present situation, talking about it might help us at least to recognize this experience when it is granted to us, and give us courage to let ourselves down into the depth which gratitude opens up.

We can begin by asking ourselves, "What happens when we feel spontaneously grateful?" (It is, of course, this concrete phenomenon which concerns us here, not any abstract notion.) For one thing, we experience joy. Joy is certainly there at the basis of thankfulness. But it is a special kind of joy, a joy received from another person. There is that remarkable "plus" which is added to my joy as soon as I perceive that it is given to me by another (necessarily *another*) person.

I can treat myself to a delicious meal, but the joy will not at all be the same as if someone else treats me to a meal, even though it be a little less exquisite. I can prepare a treat for myself, but by no means of mental acrobatics can I be grateful to myself; there lies the decisive difference between any other joy and the joy that gives rise to gratitude.

Gratitude refers to another, and to another as person. We cannot in the full sense be grateful to things, or to impersonal powers like life or nature, unless we conceive of them in some confused way as implicitly personal, super-personal, if you wish.

The moment we exclude explicitly the notion of personhood, gratitude ceases. And why? Because gratitude implies that the gift I receive is freely bestowed, and someone who is capable of doing me a favor is related to me in a personal way.

A joy, even though I receive it from another, does not make me grateful unless it is meant as a favor. We are quite sensitive to the difference. When you get an unusually big piece of pie in the cafeteria, you may find yourself hesitating for a moment, and only when you have discarded the possibility that this may indicate a change of policy or an oversight, you take it to be a favor worthy of a smile for the fellow that hands it to you across the counter.

It may be difficult in a given case to say whether the favor I receive was meant for me personally. But my gratitude will depend on the answer. At least the favor must be meant for a group with which I am personally identified. (When you wear a monk's habit you not infrequently receive a bigger piece of pie or some other unexpected kindness from someone you never met before and whom you will never meet again. But there, the people do mean you, insofar as you are a monk, and it is quite a different case from the painful experience of smiling back at someone only to discover that the smile was meant not for you but for someone who stood behind you.)

My intellect recognizes a gift as gift; my will acknowledges my dependence; my feelings celebrate in grateful joy.

Where does this little phenomenology of gratitude lead us? This much we can already say: gratitude springs from an insight, a recognition that something good has come to me from another person, that it is freely given to me, and meant as a favor. And the moment this recognition dawns on me, gratitude, too, spontaneously dawns in my heart: *je suis reconnaissant* — I recognize, I acknowledge, I am grateful; in French these three concepts are expressed by one and the same term.

I recognize the special quality of this joy: it is a joy freely granted me as a favor. I acknowledge my dependence, freely accepting as a gift what only another, as other, can freely give to me. And I am grateful, allowing my emotions fully to taste and to express the joy I have received, and thus I make it flow back to its source by returning thanks. I see that the whole of me is involved when I give thanks from my heart, from that center in which the human person is one: the intellect recognizes the gift as gift; the will acknowledges my dependence; the emotions, like a sounding board, give fullness to the melody of this experience.

The intellect recognizes: yes, it is true, this joy is a free gift; the will acknowledges: yes, it is good to accept my dependence; the emotions resound in gratitude, celebrating the beauty of this experience. Thus, the grateful heart, experiencing in truth, goodness, and beauty the fullness of being, finds through gratitude its own fulfillment. This is the reason why a person who cannot be wholeheartedly grateful is so pitiful a failure. Lack of gratitude always indicates some malfunctioning of intellect, will, or emotions that prevents the integration of the personality thus afflicted.

It may be that my intellect insists on suspicion and does not allow me to recognize any favor as favor. Selflessness cannot be proved. Reasoning about another person's motives can only take me to the point where mere intellect must yield to faith, to trust in the other, which is a gesture no longer of the intellect alone but of the whole heart. Or it may be that my proud will refuses to acknowledge my dependence on another, thus paralyzing the heart before it can rise to give thanks. Or it may be that the scar tissue of hurt feelings no longer allows my full emotional response. My longing for pure selflessness, for pure gratitude, may be so deep and so much in discrepancy with what I have experienced in the past that I give in to despair. And who am I anyway? Why should selfless love be wasted on me? Am I worthy of it? No, I am not. To face this fact, to realize my unworthiness, and yet to open myself through hope to love, this is the root of all human wholeness and holiness, the very core of the integrating gesture of thanksgiving. However, this inner gesture of gratitude can only come to itself when it finds expression.

Gratitude is a passage from suspicion to trust, from isolation to give and take, from independence to interdependence.

Expression of thanks is an integral part of gratitude, no less important than the recognition of the gift and the acknowledgment of my dependence. Think of the helplessness we experience when we do not know whom to thank for an anonymous gift. Only when my thanks are expressed and accepted is the circle of giving and thanksgiving closed and a mutual exchange established between giver and receiver.

However, the closed circle is not a well-chosen image for what happens here. We could rather compare this exchange to a spiral in which the giver receives thanksgiving, and so becomes himself receiver, and the joy of giving and receiving rises higher and higher. The mother bends down to her child in his crib and hands him a rattle. The baby recognizes the gift and returns the mother's smile. The mother, overjoyed with the childish gesture of gratitude, lifts up the child with a kiss. There is our spiral of joy. Is not the kiss a greater gift than the toy? Is not the joy it expresses greater than the joy that set our spiral in motion?

But notice that the upward movement of our spiral signifies not only that the joy has grown stronger. Rather we have passed on to something entirely new. A passage has taken place. A passage from multiplicity to unity: we start out with giver, gift, and receiver, and we arrive at the embrace of thanks expressed and thanks accepted. Who can distinguish giver and receiver in the final kiss of gratitude?

Is not gratitude a passage from suspicion to trust, from proud isolation to a humble give and take, from enslavement to false independence to self-acceptance in that dependence which liberates? Yes, gratitude is the great gesture of passage.

And this gesture of passage unites us. It unites us as human beings, for we realize that in this whole passing universe we humans are the only ones aware of its swift passing. There lies our human dignity. There lies our human task. The task of entering into the meaning of this passage (the passage which is our whole life), of celebrating its meaning through the gesture of thanksgiving.

But this gesture of passage unites us in that depth of the heart in which being human is synonymous with being religious. The essence of gratitude is self-acceptance in that dependence that liberates; but the dependence which liberates is nothing else but that religion that lies at the root of all religions, and even at the root of a truly spiritual (though misguided) rejection of all religions.

When we look at the great rites of passage that belong to our oldest heritage as humans, the religious significance of gratitude becomes clear to us. In our century anthropologists and scholars of comparative religion have re-examined these *rites de passage,* rites celebrating birth and death and the other great hours of passage through the human life. Sacrifice in one form or another belongs to the core of these rites. And this is understandable, for sacrifice itself is the prototype of all rites of passage.

The moment we take a closer look at the basic features common to the various forms of sacrificial rites, we are struck by the perfect parallel between the structure of gratitude as a gesture of the human heart and the inner structure of sacrifice. In both cases a passage takes place. In both cases the gesture rises from the joyful recognition of the gift received, culminates in the acknowledgment of the receiver's dependence on the giver, and finds its accomplishment in an external expression of thanks which unites giver and receiver, be it in the form of a conventional handshake of gratitude, or in a sacrificial meal.

Think, for example, of the sacrifice of first fruits, almost certainly the most ancient sacrificial rite. Even where we find it in its simplest and most primitive form the rite clearly displays the pattern we discovered. Let us take, for example, the Chenchu, a tribe in Southern India, belonging to one of the most ancient cultural strata not only of India but of the whole world. What happens when a Chenchu returning from a food-gathering expedition in the jungle casts a choice morsel of food into the bush and accompanies this sacrifice with a prayer to the deity worshipped as mistress of the jungle, giver of its products? "Our mother," he says, "by your kindness we have found. Without it we receive nothing. We offer you many thanks."

Thousands of similar rites have been observed among the most primitive peoples. But this example (recorded by Christoph von Fuerer Haimendorf, who did field work among the Chenchu) stands out for its crystal-clear structure. Each sentence of the simple prayer accompanying this offering corresponds, in fact, to one of our three phases of gratitude. "Our mother, by your kindness we have found": the recognition of a favor received; "without it we receive nothing": the acknowledgment of dependence; and "we offer you many thanks": the expression of gratitude that makes the original joy over the favor received rise to a higher level.

And what the prayer expresses under three aspects, the rite expresses in one gesture: the hunter who offers a piece of his quarry to the deity expresses thereby that he appreciates the goodness of the gift received, and that through the symbolic sharing of the gift he somehow enters into communion with the giver.

So striking, in fact, is the correspondence between social gestures of gratitude and religious gestures of sacrifice that one might tend to mistake the food offerings of the Chenchu and similar examples for a mere transposition of social conventions into a religious key. However, there is no simple correlation between the one and the other. Both are rooted in the depth of the heart, but they expand in two different directions.

Human religious awareness comes to itself in the very gesture of our sacrificial rites, just as our awareness of human solidarity comes to itself when we find gestures to express thanks to one another.

We look at life and sees that it comes to us from a Source far beyond our reach. We look at life and see that it is good — good for us: and from the firm ground of these two intellectual insights the heart dares to leap to a third insight that surpasses mere reasoning: the insight that all good comes to me as a free gift from the Source of Life. This leap of faith surpasses the gropings of the intellect, because it is a gesture of the whole person, very much like the trust one puts in a friend.

Gratefulness and sacrifice are two expressions of one inner gesture.

Now, the moment I recognize life as a gift, and myself as recipient, my dependence is brought home to me, and this confronts me with a decision. Just as in the social sphere I can refuse to acknowledge dependence, and lock myself up in the loneliness of pride, so in the religious dimension I can adopt a stance of proud independence towards the very Source of Life. And the temptation is strong to close my eyes to the ridiculousness of this posture. For dependence in the religious context implies more than the give and take of human interdependence; it implies willing obedience to a divine guidance. But my petty pride finds it hard to swallow this.

(It is here, incidentally, that the violence of many sacrificial rites has its root. We cannot do justice to this aspect now, but we may note in passing that violent sacrificial rites are meaningful as an expression of that violence which we must do to ourselves before our hearts, enslaved by self-will, can enter into the freedom of loving obedience.) The one who kills an animal in sacrifice expresses by this gesture complete readiness to die rather than stop short of the ultimate goal of this rite of passage. Since the goal is union between the human and the divine, a union of wills must precede it; the human will must become obedient. But the death of self-will is only the negative aspect of obedience; its positive aspect is a new birth to true life and joy. Upon the immolation follows the joy of the sacrificial banquet.

We should not overstress submission when we speak of obedience. Of much greater importance is its positive aspect: alertness to the secret signs pointing the way towards true joy. (I call them secret signs because they are intimately personal hints, at moments when we are most truly ourselves.) "We, unlike birds of passage, are not informed," says Rilke in the *Duino Elegies*. Our passage is not predetermined by instinct. All we are given are inklings like that stirring of gratitude in our hearts, and the freedom to follow these inklings.

Obedience is the homing instinct of the human heart. Detachment frees our wings, so we can soar.

To the extent to which we have forfeited this freedom, detachment is necessary. Obedience is our alertness, our *disponibilité,* our readiness to follow the homing impulse of the heart in its upward flight. Detachment liberates the wings of our heart so that we can rise to the grateful enjoyment of life in all its fullness. We must open our hand and let loose what we hold before we can receive the new gifts that every moment offers us. Detachment and obedience are merely means; the goal is joy.

If we would understand moral sacrifice in this positive way we would also understand ritual sacrifice, which is its expression. Neither of the two is that grim thing into which it is sometimes distorted. The pattern of both is the passage of thanksgiving. The accomplishment of both is the joy of our union with that which transcends us. This is expressed in the sacrificial banquet in which the rite of sacrifice culminates. This joyful meal presupposes the acceptance of our thanksgiving by the Giver. It is the embrace which unites the one who gave the gift and the one who gives thanks for it.

(Let us remember, by the way, that in the religious context, God is always the giver: we the thanks-givers. Only in the far less original context of magic can this relation deteriorate to some sort of commercial transaction or even to human effort to extort favors from super-human powers. But magic and ritualism are dead-end roads of the heart; they do not concern us here.)

What does concern us is the fact that our own experience of gratitude is closely related to a universal religious phenomenon, to sacrifice, which lies at the very root of religion. And once we have grasped the root, we can find access to religion in all its aspects. The whole history of religion can, in fact, be understood as the working out in all its implications of that sacrificial gesture that we ourselves experience as often as gratitude rises in our hearts.

Jewish religion, for example, begins with the implicit conviction that we would not be human unless we offered sacrifice, and leads up to the explicit awareness that "only those who offer themselves as sacrifice deserve to be called human" (Rabbi Israel of Rizin, who died in 1850). We have a parallel in Hinduism where an early Vedic text sees man as "the one animal capable of bringing sacrifice" (*Satapata Brahmanah* VII, 5, 2, 23), and the development culminates in a passage from the *Chandogya Upanishad* (III, 16, 1): "Verily, a person is a sacrifice." Does not our own experience show us that as human persons we find our full integrity only in the sacrificial gesture of gratefulness?

And even to the "thou shalt love" (which is in one form or another the mature fruit of every religion) does our experience of gratitude give us access. But just as the root repelled us at first by its apparent crudeness, so this fruit of religion makes us draw back from the contradiction it seems to contain. How can love be commanded? How can there be an obligation to love? Love is not love at all unless it is gratuitous. What we experience in the context of gratitude provides us with a clue: a favor we do to another remains a favor, remains gratuitous, even though our heart tells us that we ought to do it, that we ought to be generous, ought to pardon. And why? Because we belong together in a deep solidarity that the heart discerns. We belong together, because together we are obligated to a reality that transcends us.

Christ's word comes to mind: "If you are offering your gift at the altar, and there you remember that your brother has something against you, leave your gift there before the altar, and go. First make peace with your brother, then come and offer your gift" (Mt. 5:24). This is in perfect conformity with the tradition of Israel's prophets who insisted that true sacrifice is thanksgiving, that true immolation is obedience, that the true meaning of the sacrificial meal is mercy, *hesed*, the covenant, love, which binds men and women to one another by binding them as one community to God.

What is rejected is empty ritualism, not ritual. Thanksgiving, mercy, obedience are not to replace ritual, but to give it its full meaning. Indeed, man's whole life is to become a sacred ritual of thanksgiving, the whole universe a sacrifice. When the prophet Zechariah says that "on that day" (the day of the Messiah) "every pot and pan in Jerusalem and Judah shall be sacred to the Lord of hosts, so that all who sacrifice may come and use them," the implication is that there is nothing on earth that cannot become a vessel filled with thanksgiving and so lifted up to God.

It is this universal *Eucharistia*, this cosmic celebration of a thanksgiving sacrifice that forms the heart of the Christian message. Thus the worldwide intuition of human hearts that the spiral of thanksgiving is the dynamic pattern of all reality finds its typically Christian formulation in the belief that even within the absolute oneness of God there is room for an eternal exchange of giving and thanksgiving, a spiral of joy. Within the one and undivided Godhead, there is still room for the Father's total self-giving to the Son and the Son's self-giving in total thanksgiving to the Father. And Love, the gift, eternally exchanged between Father and Son is herself, personal and divine, the Holy Spirit of Thanksgiving.

Creation and redemption are simply an overflow of this divine *perichorese*, this inner-trinitarian dance, an overflow into what of itself is nothingness. God the Son becomes the Son of Man in obedience to the Father, so as to unite through his sacrifice in merciful love all God's children with one another and with the Father, leading them back in the Spirit of Thanksgiving to that eternal embrace in which "God will be all in all" (1 Co. 13:28). "Whatever exists, exists through sacrifice" (*Sat. Brah.* XI, 2, 3, 6). And note: this is a Hindu insight! The whole cosmos is being renewed moment by moment through sacrifice: brought back to its source through thanksgiving and received anew as gift in all its primordial freshness. But this universal sacrifice is possible only because the one God is Giver, Gift, and Thanksgiver.

To the extent to which we have given room in our hearts to gratitude, we all have a share in this reality, by whatever name we may call it. (It is a reality that we shall never fully take hold of. All that matters is that we let it take hold of us.) All that matters is that we enter into that passage of gratitude and sacrifice, the passage which leads us to integrity within ourselves, to concord with one another and to union with the very Source of Life. For "...this is all that matters: that we can bow, take a deep bow. Just that, Just that."